The Interior Castle

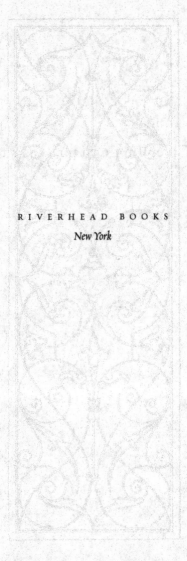

RIVERHEAD BOOKS

New York

The
Interior Castle

❧

Saint Teresa of Avila

NEW TRANSLATION AND
INTRODUCTION BY MIRABAI STARR

RIVERHEAD BOOKS
Published by the Penguin Group
Penguin Group (USA) Inc.
375 Hudson Street, New York, New York 10014, USA

Penguin Group (Canada), 90 Eglinton Avenue East, Suite 700, Toronto,
Ontario M4P 2Y3, Canada (a division of Pearson Penguin Canada Inc.)
Penguin Group Ltd., 80 Strand, London WC2R 0RL, England
Penguin Group Ireland, 25 St. Stephen's Green, Dublin 2, Ireland (a division of Penguin Books Ltd.)
Penguin Group (Australia), 250 Camberwell Road, Camberwell, Victoria 3124, Australia
(a division of Pearson Australia Group Pty. Ltd.)
Penguin Books India Pvt. Ltd., 11 Community Centre, Panchsheel Park, New Delhi—110 017, India
Penguin Group (NZ), 67 Apollo Drive, Rosedale, Auckland 0632, New Zealand
(a division of Pearson New Zealand Ltd.)
Penguin Books (South Africa) (Pty.) Ltd., 24 Sturdee Avenue, Rosebank, Johannesburg 2196,
South Africa

Penguin Books Ltd., Registered Offices: 80 Strand, London WC2R 0RL, England

The publisher does not have any control over and does not assume any responsibility for
author or third-party websites or their content.

Translation and introduction copyright © 2003 by Mirabai Starr
Cover design by Aliza Dzik
Front cover art: Remedios Varo, *Spiral Transit* © Walter Gruen Berger / The Estate of
Remedios Varo
Interior text design by Amanda Dewey

First Riverhead hardcover edition: June 2003
First Riverhead trade paperback edition: July 2004
Riverhead trade paperback ISBN: 978-1-59448-005-8

The Library of Congress has catalogued the Riverhead hardcover edition as follows:

Teresa of Avila, Saint, 1515–1582.
[Castillo interior. English]
   The interior castle / Teresa of Avila; new translation and introduction by Mirabai Starr.
      p.   cm
   ISBN 978-1-57322-248-8
   1. Spiritual life—Catholic Church—Early works to 1800.   I. Starr, Mirabai.   II. Title.
   BX2179.T4C4413   2003
   2002037086
   248.4'82—dc21

PRINTED IN THE UNITED STATES OF AMERICA

20   19   18   17   16   15   14   13   12   11

To my mother, Susanna Starr, with all my love

ACKNOWLEDGMENTS

To the circle of family and friends who created a sanctuary for me to write this translation in the wake of the sudden death of my beloved daughter, Jenny, I offer my boundless gratitude. The refuge of this work saved me.

Thanks to Susanna Starr, for knowing from experience what it is to lose a child and for preparing a warm and comfortable writing retreat for me in the valley and quietly feeding me on every level so I could work. Thanks to Amy Starr and Roy Starr, for guiding and protecting me on our odyssey through the wilderness of New York City as I encountered the publishing world. Thanks to Daniela Starr Whitehorse, who has flowered into the quintessential devoted daughter and a beautiful young mother in her own right. Thanks to Bette Little, for being a living example of a strong, independent woman with vast heart.

I am deeply grateful to my women's writing group, which has held me so tenderly through my grieving and my writing: Elaine Sutton; Susan Berman; Linda Fair; Adair Ferdon; Lorie Levison; Tania Casselle; Diane Chase; Jean Kenin. Heartfelt thanks to Ted and Marcella Wiard at the Golden Willow Retreat. Thank you, Fr. Bill McNichols, for your continued faith in the divine rightness of this Hindu/Buddhist/Jew translating the Catholic saints.

Special thanks to Bobbi Shapiro, who read every word of the manuscript as it unfolded and offered the most helpful feedback of all: how the teachings of a sixteenth-century Spanish nun apply to those of us on a spiritual path today; to Cathleen Medwick, whose expertise in Teresian studies is extraordinary, exceeded only by her heartfulness and generosity; and to Sharon Salzberg, for mentoring me in the business of spiritual literature and the cultivation of bright faith, against all odds.

Thanks to my agent, Peter Rubie, for his wise advice and sense of humor; to my editor at Riverhead, Amy Hertz, for her gentle touch and flashing insight; and to Amy's superhero assistant, Marc Haeringer, for his unwavering kindness, startling intelligence, and skillful handling of impossible details; and to Timothy Luke Meyer, copyeditor at Riverhead, for his breadth of knowledge and depth of caring.

I offer humble thanks to my spiritual mentors: Saint Teresa of Avila, Saint John of the Cross, Neem Karoli Baba, and Jenny Starr, whose guidance throughout this writing has been continuously tangible.

Finally, my deepest appreciation goes to Ganga Das (Jeff Little), who married me in the middle of all this and constantly reminds me that "all will be well and all will be well, and all manner of things will be well."

CONTENTS

The Interior Castle

INTRODUCTION

The Calling

There is a secret place. A radiant sanctuary. As real as your own kitchen. More real than that. Constructed of the purest elements. Overflowing with the ten thousand beautiful things. Worlds within worlds. Forests, rivers. Velvet coverlets thrown over featherbeds, fountains bubbling beneath a canopy of stars. Bountiful forests, universal libraries. A wine cellar offering an intoxication so sweet you will never be sober again. A clarity so complete you will never again forget.

This magnificent refuge is inside you. Enter. Shatter the darkness that shrouds the doorway. Step around the poisonous vipers that slither at your feet, attempting to throw you off your course. Be bold. Be humble. Put away the incense and forget the incantations they taught you. Ask no permission from the authorities. Slip away. Close your eyes and follow your breath to the still place that leads to the invisible path that leads you home.

Listen. Softly, the One you love is calling. Listen. At first, you will only hear traces of his voice. Love letters he drops for you in hiding places. In the sound of your baby laughing, in your boyfriend telling you a dream, in a book about loving-kindness, in the sun dipping down below the horizon and a peacock's tail of purple and orange clouds unfolding behind it, in the nameless sorrow that fills your heart when you wake in the night and remember that the world has gone to war and you are powerless to break up the fight. Let the idle chatter between friends drop down to what matters. Listen. Later his voice will come closer. A whisper you're almost sure is meant for you fading in and out of the cacophony of thoughts, clearer in the silent space between them. Listen. His call is flute music, far away. Coming closer.

Be brave and walk through the country of your own wild heart. Be gentle and know that you know nothing. Be mindful and remember that every moment can be a prayer. Melting butter, scrambling eggs, lifting fork to mouth, praising God. Typing your daughter's first short story, praising God. Losing your temper and your dignity with someone you love, praising God. Balancing ecstasy with clear thinking, self-control with self-abandon. Be still. Listen. Keep walking.

What a spectacular kingdom you have entered! Befriending the guards and taming the lions at the gates. Sliding through a crack in the doorway on your prayer rug. Crossing the moat between this world and that, walking on water if you have to, because this is your rightful place. That is your Beloved reclining in the innermost chamber, waiting for you, offering wine from a bottle with your crest on the label. Explore. Rest if you have to, but don't go to sleep. Head straight for his arms.

And when you have dismissed the serpents of vanity and greed, conquered the lizards of self-importance, and lulled the monkey mind to sleep, your steps will be lighter. When you have given up everything to make a friend a cup of tea and tend her broken heart, stood up against the violation of innocent children and their fathers and mothers, made conscious choices to live simply and honor the earth, your steps will be lighter. When you have grown still on purpose while everything around you is asking for your chaos, you will find the doors between every room of this interior castle thrown open, the path home to your true love unobstructed after all.

No one else controls access to this perfect place. Give yourself your own unconditional permission to go there. Absolve yourself of missing the mark again and again. Believe the incredible truth that the Beloved has chosen for his dwelling place the core of your own being because that is the single most beautiful place in all of creation. Waste no time. Enter the center of your soul.

An Epic Life

In her Prelude to *Middlemarch*, the nineteenth-century femi-
nist writer George Eliot invokes Saint Teresa as a perfect
example of a woman who stumbled upon the rare grace to
actually live out the exalted calling of her spirit. "Teresa's passionate, ideal nature," writes Eliot, "demanded an epic life."

It is now common knowledge that Teresa of Jesus, born
Teresa de Ahumada y Cepeda in 1515, came from a family
with hidden Jewish roots. Recoiling from the Inquisition of
fifteenth-century Spain, Teresa's wealthy Jewish grandfather,
Juan Sanchez, purchased the status of *hidalgo*, a titled gentle-
man, to buy his children access to the noble classes so that
they could marry well. But this was only after Juan Sanchez
had discovered that he and his family were under suspicion
by the Inquisition for secretly practicing Judaism in their
home. Many *conversas* were actually crypto-Jews who publicly
professed strict adherence to Christian dogma and privately
went right ahead practicing their ancestral faith.

Everyone knew that the punishment for such crimes
could be deadly. So Juan Sanchez decided to confess before he
could be condemned. His diluted sentence was more humili-
ating than life threatening. He and his children were marched
through the streets of Toledo for seven Fridays in a row, forced
to wear costumes of bright yellow emblazoned with a flaming
cross and snakes. Denouncing the Sabbath of their people,
they were required to kneel in every church, chapel, and shrine

in the city. The job of the townspeople was to throw stones and spit and hurl verbal abuses at the nasty Jews.

Teresa's father, Alonso Sanchez de Cepeda, was the youngest son of Juan Sanchez. Stung by this early experience of public mortification, Alonso focused on cultivating a life of status and prestige for himself and his own family. At the end of his life, through the inspiration of his gifted daughter Teresa, Alonso's own passionate love for God was enkindled.

Early in his first marriage, Alonso's young wife, Catalina, died suddenly, leaving him with two small children. He married her fourteen-year-old cousin, Beatriz Davila de Ahumada, who bore him nine more children before dying in childbirth by the age of thirty. Teresa was twelve when she lost her mother, and she was devastated by her death. Beatriz had been unusually close to her children. She used to read to them under the apple trees from the chivalrous romance novels popular at the time. Teresa appealed to the Virgin Mary to please be her mother now, a prayer that burned in her heart for the rest of her life.

But first, Teresa spent some time out of control. It appears that she took advantage of what must have been an overwhelming domestic predicament for poor Alonso. Teresa adored her father, but she was a wild child. She swept up various siblings and neighboring cousins on her adventures. Harmless enough when Teresa and her companions were children off to the borderlands to challenge the Moors, these exploits grew more serious once they reached adolescence.

When she was sixteen, it was discovered that Teresa's liaison with a certain boy to whom she happened to be distantly related had grown more intimate than was socially acceptable. It is not clear what exactly unfolded between the beautiful and vivacious Teresa and her smitten cousin. While the late Victoria Lincoln calls Teresa's virginity into question in her biography titled *Teresa: A Woman,* her sin may have been as simple as sitting in the garden with a boy, unchaperoned.

Teresa herself refers obliquely to the mischievous behaviors of her youth, chuckling when she is ludicrously accused of certain sexual indiscretions in her sixties while the actual crimes of her girlhood managed to fade into obscurity! Regardless of the precise degree to which this forbidden romance had progressed, the consequence was classic: Teresa was banished to a nunnery. The hope was that a convent education would not only straighten out the wayward girl but would remove her from the sphere of temptation and allow the neighborhood focus to shift to fresh topics of interest.

To her own amazement, the high-spirited Teresa actually began to find herself developing a taste for the life of quiet prayer to which she had been exiled. She started to search her soul to see if she was genuinely destined for a monastic vocation, and she asked the nuns to pray for guidance on her behalf. After a process of rigorous self-inquiry, she arrived at this answer: it had to be better than marriage!

This was not a simple solution. There were a thousand things about the Augustinian convent Teresa abhorred. Besides, all the other nuns seemed to be so much more deeply moved by God than she was. In choir, one or another smitten girl would regularly weep at the feet of the Lord while Teresa couldn't squeeze out a single holy tear. But the truth was, she feared for her soul. Teresa knew her own nature. She was determined not to ever again compromise her father's honor with her own indiscreet romantic entanglements. She still found social discourse to be seductive. She couldn't help but suspect that this compulsion of hers to get people to like her would ultimately send her to hell.

To her dismay, Teresa's father did not agree to her plan. His temporary solution to his daughter's troubling behavior had backfired. Why couldn't she just cheerfully wait out the stir of gossip in the safety of the cloister and then come home and find a decent husband like other girls? Witnessing the death of her beloved mother as a result of unrelenting child-birth may well have served at least as a partial deterrent against choosing the path of family. But Teresa's calling to a spiritual life was probably higher than that.

"Her flame," Eliot writes of Teresa's rejection of a domestic life, "quickly burned up that light fuel; and, fed from within, soared after some illimitable satisfaction, some object which would never justify weariness, which would reconcile self-despair with the rapturous consciousness of life beyond self."

Teresa's decision to renounce the world coincided with a rapid plunge in physical health. She began suffering from fainting spells and inexplicable fevers. On more than one occasion, she was forced to take a leave of absence from the convent and return to her father's house to recuperate. It was during one of these interludes that Teresa encountered teachings on silent prayer in the books that her uncle Pedro had her read aloud to him. Her attraction to a contemplative life deepened, and she finally convinced her father to support her decision to take vows.

This profession, however, did not eradicate Teresa's troubles in one holy stroke. Her body continued to take her on a wild ride of undiagnosed attacks. At one point, she even suffered a fit of paralysis from which it took many months to fully recover. In fact, Teresa spent her entire life battling a throbbing head, inflamed joints, and rocketing temperatures.

But the dangers for Teresa weren't only unfolding on a physical level. The worldly temptations she was so eager to leave behind followed her to the monastery. Visitors were invited to the convent parlor on weekends to discuss the condition of their souls with the nuns. Teresa was the natural star of this show. A skilled conversationalist and inveterate flirt, she managed to compel everyone around her to vie for a piece of her attention—especially men. Before she realized that she herself was becoming a victim of her own dubious gifts of seduction, the beautiful young nun once again grew perilously intimate with a man. She caught herself just in time to save her reputation and her mortal soul. Something, she reckoned, had to change.

Finally, after yet another bout of mysterious illness, Teresa was recovering at her uncle's farm in the country when Pedro, sensing her turmoil, gave her a copy of *The Third Spiritual Alphabet,* by Francisco de Osuna. This particular treatise on contemplative prayer helped serve as a catalyst for a radical shift in her inner life. "What Osuna taught and Teresa learned with alacrity," writes Cathleen Medwick in her beautiful biography *Teresa of Avila: The Progress of a Soul*, "is something that might be defined as a spiritual fitness: a kind of alert praying, a limbering up and bracing of the faculties to weather God's onslaught of love."

As Teresa dedicated herself to the cultivation of interior silence and began to grow in wisdom, her soul unfolding and flowering, her health continued to decline. At one point, she slipped into a coma and was about to be pronounced dead when she suddenly pried open her eyes beneath the wax that had already been pressed upon her lids in preparation for burial. Her recovery was deemed miraculous, and the passion of her devotion to her God deepened.

Still, Teresa's path was not yet marked by the religious fireworks and divinely altered states of consciousness for which she was to become so famous. In fact, though she was diligent in her spiritual practice, her inner life was rather ordinary for the next two decades.

Then, suddenly, near her fortieth year, God-states started to descend like a monsoon on the parched landscape of Teresa's soul. It began with an ordinary day in which the unsuspecting nun was strolling to the oratory. A statue of Christ, known as the "Ecce Homo," which someone had placed in the corridor, caught her eye. The next thing she knew, Teresa was prostrate on the floor, sobbing. The image of the suffering redeemer unlocked decades of remorse and longing. The flow of tears seemed to serve as a purifying stream, washing away all her pent-up agitation. When at last she rose to her feet again, she felt refreshed, renewed, even reborn.

From then on, Teresa experienced a relentless series of supernatural states. Visions of the resurrected Christ, his Blessed Mother, and various saints were punctuated by spiritual voices in which specific messages were transmitted, such as, "Now I want you to speak not with men but with angels."

Teresa understood what this meant. She plunged into a life of unceasing prayer with all the zeal of a convert. Her raptures were frequent and famous. Sometimes she entered into trancelike states that paralyzed her for hours, and she seemed to stop breathing. When these things happened in public, Teresa found them terribly embarrassing. Legend tells it that as Teresa was in the choir singing among her sisters one day, she began to levitate. When the other nuns started to whisper and point, Teresa lowered her gaze and realized that she had risen several inches above the stone floor. "Put me down!" she demanded of God. And he did.

Once, when the Christ child appeared and asked her who she was, she replied, "I am Teresa of Jesus. Who are you?"

"I am Jesus of Teresa," he said.

Perhaps the most influential of Teresa's mystical moments was immortalized in marble by the Italian sculptor Gian Lorenzo Bernini. He called it *Saint Teresa in Ecstasy*. In this unabashedly sensual image, we see the nun swooning blissfully backward while a clearly delighted androgynous angel plunges a flaming sword into her, leaving her on fire with love for God.

This experience has come to be known as the "transverberation" and it occurred repeatedly over a sustained period of Teresa's life. Each time the blade was withdrawn, Teresa felt as if her very entrails were being pulled out with it. "The pain is so severe," Teresa writes in her autobiography, "it made me moan. The sweetness of the intense pain is so extreme, there is no wanting it to end, and the soul isn't satisfied with anything less than God." She had to admit that "the body has a large share" in this agonizing ecstasy.

As word began to spread about Teresa's extraordinary experiences, the eyes of the Inquisition turned toward the middle-aged nun. But Teresa's scrutiny of her own states was at least as severe as theirs. Fruitlessly, Teresa spent years seeking wise counsel to help her determine once and for all whether her visions, locutions, and raptures came from God or from the devil, or maybe even from mental pathology, all expressions of which at that time were lumped under the single heading of "melancholy."

Teresa seemed to find her spiritual gifts more humbling than exalting. While she praised God continuously for blessing "a common woman" with such glorious tastes of his love, she remained equally devoted to the sanctity of the ordinary. Provisions were often scarce in convent life and Teresa enjoyed cooking and eating. "God," Teresa would say, "lives also among the pots and pans." Once, upon being politely questioned about the obvious pleasure she took in food, Teresa was said to have commented, "When praying, pray. When eating partridge, eat partridge," and returned with gusto to her meal. "God save me from pious nuns," was a prayer Teresa was heard to mumble frequently under her breath.

By the time Teresa of Avila met John of the Cross, one of the few men she ever seemed to have recognized as being worthy of guiding her soul, she was learning to balance the inner life with the outer, to keep her ecstatic impulses in check when it was time to tend to the business of religious reform. Frustrated by her observations of the lazy slide of an Order founded originally on the ideals of simplicity and silence, Teresa took it upon herself to spearhead a return to a path of poverty and contemplative prayer in the Carmelite community.

The twenty-five-year-old priest John of the Cross stood barely five feet tall, with the smoldering eyes and dark brown skin that betokened his mixed Jewish and Moorish heritage. John was disillusioned by the same unholy behaviors that were bothering Teresa. He was, in fact, on his way to the mountains to live as a hermit when the fifty-two-year-old nun waylaid him, converting him to her cause. Together with Fr. Jerónimo Gracián they founded convents and monasteries throughout Spain, dedicated to the uncompromising spiritual principles of their reform. Their movement was called Discalced, or Barefoot Carmelites, reflecting their commitment to the simple values symbolized by the hemp sandals they wore even in winter. It was only a year before Teresa's death at age sixty-seven that the Discalced Carmelites were finally sanctioned as an official Order of the Catholic Church.

Like two hot-headed lovers, the aging celibate nun Teresa and the celibate young priest John had a passionate and tumultuous connection. Many years into their relationship, John, a natural renunciate, came to the conclusion that he was overly attached to Teresa and so he systematically burned a treasury of letters documenting their friendship. Teresa both revered John's penetrating insight and resented his unapologetic critique of her dramatic spiritual episodes.

Still, John's questions were among the few Teresa ever seemed to seriously ponder, while Teresa's vision of a contemplative path became the mission of the rest of his life. This dedication resulted in his capture by the mainstream Carmelites only three days after Teresa finished writing *The Interior Castle.* The angry monks imprisoned their brother in a dark tower and tortured him for nine months. On the verge of death, John miraculously escaped captivity, finding sanctuary in one of Teresa's Discalced convents, where he composed his mystical masterpiece, *Dark Night of the Soul.*

Throughout her career as both a mystic and a reformer, Teresa was ever-vigilant of the looming presence of the Inquisition. For the most part, she was successful in deterring them through the skillful wielding of a gifted mind and unmitigated charisma. Her legacy is staggering. During the last two decades of her life, in spite of severe health challenges,

Teresa managed to travel all over the countryside by carriage, founding seventeen Discalced Carmelite houses, and writing multiple volumes of what have come to be considered some of the most significant classics in the history of spiritual literature in between expeditions.

On one particularly grueling trip, Teresa and her nuns were attempting to cross a raging river with their donkey cart when a cable broke and washed away their supplies. Exasperated, Teresa withdrew to meditate under a tree. There, she heard the voice of God reassuring her that this hardship was a sign of his loving friendship. "Well, no wonder you have so few friends, then!" Teresa grumbled in reply.

Against the fervently expressed wishes of John of the Cross, who feared for his mentor's well-being, Teresa made the last journey of her life at the end of 1582. On her way to found a convent in the north, Teresa was sidetracked by a message from a duchess demanding the presence of the saintly nun at the impending birth of her first grandchild. It was a harrowing trip. Harsh weather and brutal conditions battered Teresa so badly that by the time she reached her destination she excused herself and went right to bed.

Teresa never got up again. Legend holds it that with her last breath, Teresa uttered these words: "Beloved, it's time to move on. Well, then, may your will be done. Oh, my Lord and my Spouse, the hour that I have longed for has come. It's time for us to meet one another."

At that moment, they say, a white dove lifted into flight from under the saint's covers. A tree whose leaves had all dropped burst suddenly into blossom as if it were April and not October. A mortally ill nun was instantaneously cured. And a radiant light streamed into the death chamber while the perfume of lilies filled the air.

After that, a long drama unfolded around Teresa's unconventional sanctity. Was she genuinely holy or merely hysterical? Was it true that even after two years her body had not decomposed and still smelled of lilies? Couldn't it be argued that this woman perhaps loved God a little too much? While the Inquisition challenged her as vigorously after her death as they had throughout her adult life, Teresa's devotees prevailed and she was finally canonized in 1622.

For five centuries women have looked to Teresa of Avila as a role model for a strong, outspoken, independent female of passionate convictions and lofty ideals made manifest. Her love for her neighbor, especially her nuns, was legendary; she lived Christ's teachings on the path of the heart. Men and women alike continue to be dazzled by her brilliance, their hearts broken open by her compassion.

The Language of Longing

There are uncountable fruits for the contemporary spiritual seeker to harvest from the writings of Teresa of Avila. But that same seeker can't help but wonder why this brilliant mystic, long respected as an inspiration to feminists and venerated as a saint, constantly disparaged herself. Not only did she belittle herself in her writings, but she included all women in her declarations of inferiority.

I believe there were at least a couple of reasons for the attitude of self-deprecation that strikes such a dissonant chord in Teresa's otherwise bold discourse on the spiritual path. The most obvious is that this stance might well have saved her life.

From the moment she had her first mystical rapture to the night she drew her last breath, Teresa lived in fear of the Spanish Inquisition. Hyper-alert to the threat of the Protestant Reformation, Inquisitors were constantly on the lookout for unorthodox practices. A fringe group of Catholics, known as the *Alumbrados,* was gaining in popularity. This was a movement that emphasized the cultivation of ecstatic states over formal prayer, which cast Teresa's raptures in an even more suspicious light. Her life was characterized by the struggle to balance the radical nature of her personal truth with the political discretion required to prevent her from being condemned as a heretic. Nowhere else is this struggle reflected more dramatically than in her final masterpiece, *The Interior Castle.* By the end of her life, Teresa had learned her lesson. If she didn't put herself down first, the Inquisition was likely to do it for her, and not just with words.

For this reason also Teresa continuously refers to herself in her writing as "a certain person," as if this would disguise her identity. This phrase couldn't be more transparent. It is a case of the Emperor's New Clothes, under which the naked Teresa boldly and brightly shines.

Though she came from a privileged family, Teresa was never formally educated. She was a woman, destined for one of two possible paths: devoted wife and mother or pious nun. Her innate wisdom was constantly being challenged by the *letrados,* men of learning (or "half-learned men," as Teresa sometimes referred to them, whom she considered to be the most dangerous and tiresome men of all).

But because these were the leading characters in the prevailing power drama and Teresa required their approval for the safety and survival of her reform, she made sure that she regularly told them what they wanted to hear. "Who am I to speak about such lofty things as prayer?" she wonders demurely, between sublimely expressed passages on the inner life: "Nothing but a stupid woman."

Contemporary feminists might be tempted to give up on Teresa in disgust after reading one too many of these shrill disclaimers, but I urge readers to be mindful of the historical context in which they arose. Teresa had the double disadvantage of having a *converso* heritage and being a woman in a world dominated by Roman Catholic men. Teresa was probably suffering far less from a case of fatally low self-esteem than she was in danger of losing her life to ideological persecution.

On the other hand, I believe that there was an element of authenticity in Teresa's cultivated modesty. Knowing full well that she was gifted with uncommon wit and charm, Teresa was engaged in a lifelong battle against vanity and temptation. She considers the most important dwelling of the interior castle to be the chamber of self-knowledge and humility. Over and over again, she stresses to her nuns that if they are graced with the gift of spiritual raptures, they should not consider themselves to be any more special than anyone else but instead use these blessings as an opportunity for praising God and recognizing the insignificance of the separate self.

Still, I confess that I took the liberty as Teresa's most recent English-language translator to soften some of her more loaded religious vocabulary. In keeping with my rendering of *Dark Night of the Soul,* by Teresa of Avila's beloved spiritual companion, John of the Cross, I opted to minimize references to the inherent wickedness of human beings and replace such terms as "sin" and "evil" with "missing the mark," "imperfection," "unconsciousness," "limitations," and "negativity." "Mortal sin" is "grave error." I call "hell" "the underworld" and the "devil" the "spirit of evil." What I name the "three divine Persons" in the seventh dwelling is what Teresa refers to as the "Holy Trinity." Sometimes I replace "Lord" with "Beloved" because I truly believe Teresa's lifelong devotion to her God is more accurately reflected in this mystical term, which bypasses patriarchal connotations. I have preserved the convention of Spanish mysticism to refer to the soul (*el alma*) in the feminine.

The most fervent prayer of anyone translating any genius must be something like, "Please let me be so immersed in the spirit of this work that I convey the message truly, across the vast chasm of time and space, language and culture.

May the stylistic and philosophical choices I make be true to that spirit." This prayer was certainly mine each day that I sat down at my table spread with a banquet of books. I lit the candle my daughter gave to me when I first started translating the saints, and I asked for guidance from a mystic whose masterpiece I was so brazenly rewriting in hopes of making it accessible to a contemporary circle of spiritual seekers I knew needed her. I can't help but believe that she would have approved of my boldness, if not the results.

The Vision

In her sixties, when Teresa of Avila had already lived far longer inside her own aching bones than she had ever anticipated, she was having one of those dangling conversations about the spiritual path one day with her confessor, Gracián.

"Oh, I said this so much better in the *Book of My Life!*" she lamented.

But her autobiography had long since fallen into the hands of the Spanish Inquisition. Twenty years earlier, the Inquisition had first begun to hear stories about a middle-aged Carmelite nun who, after a long and undistinguished monastic career, had suddenly begun having raptures all the time. Just what exactly was going on? they demanded. Guilelessly, Teresa wrote in great detail about the "favors" God had given her. She never suspected that telling the truth would get her into such trouble, precipitating years of heartache and stress.

"Write it again," Gracián urged her. "Only this time paint your experiences in a very general way so that nobody could prove that you're talking about your own life. Direct it to your nuns. They need these teachings. We all do."

"Is this an order?" Teresa asked ruefully, in which case her vow of obedience would compel her to comply.

"It is." Gracián smiled. Like many of the men in Teresa's life, he was in his heart as much her disciple as her superior, but by virtue of the gender roles dictated by the Catholic Church, he considered it his duty to shepherd her soul, and Teresa genuinely valued his guidance.

Talking about prayer was one thing; sitting down to write was another. In the two decades since Teresa had had her first mystical experiences, she had written a number of major books on the path of prayer, composed volumes of sacred poetry, and carried on a collection of prolific correspondences. In between writing projects, and against unimaginable odds, she had directed a revolutionary religious reform throughout Spain.

Still, Teresa's inner life had ripened immeasurably since she had written that initial account of her own spiritual story. She had to admit that she had learned a few things since then, which perhaps not only qualified her to speak of certain advanced states of prayer but actually obligated her to share her understanding with other souls who had committed themselves to the journey of awakening.

This realization did not, however, make the prospect of obeying Gracián's directive any easier. By this time, Teresa's reform was under more intense fire than ever before. And her physical health was a mess. Between dodging political bullets and enduring horrendous headaches, bouts of vertigo, and a multitude of other bodily ailments, Teresa was in no mood to write another book. All she wanted to do was sit by the fire with her spinning, then trundle off to the choir and sing to her God.

The Prologue to *The Interior Castle* is little more than a veiled complaint. "Few tasks that I have been commanded by obedience to undertake have been as difficult as this one," Teresa writes. And so she turned to the only source of help she had ever known: God. "Beloved," she prayed, "I have no idea what to say here. If you want me to do this thing, you're going to have to speak through me." Apparently, he did.

Nuns who witnessed their mother superior at work on her new book described the process as something like automatic writing. Her hands flew across the page. Her face held a sustained expression of bliss. Sometimes her eyes were not even focused on the paper but rather turned upward, as if gazing upon some invisible beauty above her. Not counting a few prolonged interruptions, Teresa produced the entire mystical masterpiece of *The Interior Castle* in around two months!

It all began with a vision the Beloved revealed to Teresa when she appealed to him for assistance. It was the image of a magnificent castle inside our own souls, at the center of which the Beloved himself dwells. Out of this vision, Teresa saw the whole book unfold in a flash. From then on, it was simply a matter of recording what she saw, peppering her report with frequent editorial outbursts about what a great God it is who has created such a masterpiece of love as the human soul.

The extraordinary thing about this castle where God lives is that it is inside of us. The journey to union with the Beloved is a journey home to the center of ourselves. "What do you think a place might be like that such a king . . . would find so delightful?" Teresa asks her sisters in chapter one. "I myself can come up with nothing as magnificent as the beauty and amplitude of a soul."

No matter how many disclaimers Teresa tosses into this book in an effort to reassure the Inquisition that she is not willfully violating the authority of the Church, nothing can dilute this powerful premise. The human soul is so glorious that God himself chooses it as his dwelling place. The path to God, then, leads us on a journey of self-discovery. To know the self is to know God. And these souls of ours, far from being odious, are perfect, beautiful, inviolable.

Not only that, but we have free access to them whenever we please. This could be a threatening concept to the Church. After all, neither ritual nor authority figures are required. All we have to do is be still and go within. No wonder contemplatives have never been popular among institutionalized religious bodies. If it hadn't been for Teresa's gift for charming Spanish inquisitors, government officials, and prospective supporters, as well as her carefully cultivated political connections in a multitude of sectors, she might just as easily have been burned at the stake as venerated as a saint.

The Innermost Chamber of God

From the center of the soul, Teresa teaches, God is calling. The driving force of our existence is our longing to find our way home to him. This quest involves passage through the seven essential chambers of the interior castle. The doorway to the castle is contemplative prayer. But entry is guarded by a host of venomous creatures whose mission is to thwart the soul's journey to union with the Beloved by distracting her with all kinds of insidious worldly temptations.

Once the soul succeeds in entering the castle, she can be sure that various nasty reptiles will sneak in behind her, persisting in their efforts to lead the soul astray. Her only hope is to cultivate a discipline of humility and self-knowledge. She must continuously remember to recognize her own limitations and praise the greatness of God.

The heat and light emanating from the innermost chamber of God to every room in the castle reaches this first dwelling only in diffuse form. Through the intentional practice of prayer, the soul herself develops the power to endure the challenges of the first dwelling and enter the second.

This is where the soul begins to learn how to tune out the clamor of the mundane world and tune into the delicate voice of God. It's not that he is speaking to her personally (that kind of intimacy comes later), but rather she hears him in the form of meaningful conversations with other souls on the path, through inspiring speeches, and through sacred literature. God's light is a little warmer and brighter here than it was in the first dwelling. There is still ample space for backsliding, but the soul that humbly perseveres in prayer will progress to the third dwelling.

At this stage, the soul has a tendency to take herself almost unbearably seriously. She is determined not to lose her way. But no matter how rigorously she practices spiritual discipline in the third dwelling, God does not seem to be forthcoming in providing the consolations she craves. Prayer begins to feel dry and empty. This aridity, Teresa reassures us, is a test of humility. If the soul can quit trying to figure God out with her mind and concentrate on feeling him with her heart, if she can learn to surrender her personal will to the inscrutable will of the Beloved, she will progress to the fourth dwelling.

What a wondrous abode this is! The fourth dwelling is the balance point between the first three dwellings, where the soul evolves through her own conscious effort, and the final three dwellings, where God takes over. It is the place where the natural and the supernatural commingle. It is the heart cave, the shining vortex out of which emanates three primal energy centers below and three sublime energy centers above. It is all about love.

"The important thing," Teresa writes, "is not to think much, but to love much, and so to do whatever best awakens us to love." In this chapter, Teresa makes a distinction between the spiritual consolations God sometimes offers to weaker souls along their journey and the divine sweetness with which he fills the soul in a state of infused prayer. Teresa names this state the Prayer of Quiet. The senses and the intellect are recollected and stilled, here.

To highlight the difference between the gratification that comes as a result of our own discipline and the grace of holy delight, Teresa draws a comparison between water that fills a basin by making its noisy path through an elaborately engineered series of aqueducts and water that fills a trough soundlesslessly from a source that springs from right inside it.

In the fifth dwelling, the soul becomes engaged to marry God. What joy! She experiences this promise through infused contemplation, which Teresa names the Prayer of Union. Here, the faculties are totally suspended. When the soul emerges from this state she is left without a shred of doubt that "she was in God and God was in her."

This is where Teresa departs momentarily from the castle imagery and introduces the metaphor of the silkworm. This ugly bug miraculously spins itself a house of the most exquisite material and then climbs inside it to die. The house, Teresa explains, is Christ, and the worm is the soul before she has been transformed by union with the Beloved into a beautiful white butterfly. Only by dying to our small separate selves can we be set free to fly home to God.

In the sixth dwelling, the soul and God get to know one another better. As they spend more time alone together, they fall more deeply in love. The soul in the sixth dwelling experiences this love as a searing wound. Sometimes the pain is expressed as unbearable longing; other times it manifests in the form of terrible physical afflictions. Sometimes the torment comes through malicious gossip and misunderstanding from people the soul had felt closest to; this kind of betrayal, says Teresa, "takes the biggest bite out of her."

Still, much of the soul's suffering in this place is infused with an ineffable happiness. Her raptures grow more frequent and intense. She recognizes that her wound comes from God, and she spontaneously prays that she never recover!

But healing comes anyway, in the seventh dwelling. The soul has arrived at last at the innermost chamber where the Beloved dwells. Now her union with him is complete. This is where the greatest of all mystical paradoxes unfolds.

When the lover at last achieves union with the object of her longing, her separate self is annihilated. Like rain falling into an infinite sea, all boundaries between the soul and God melt. Union, by definition, transcends the subject-object distinction. There is no longer any lover left to enjoy her Beloved. There is only love.

Still, says Teresa, until the beatific vision given after death, the soul must eventually recover her individuality even from this ultimate melding and return to the ordinary world. But she is forever changed. Like the Zen description of the state of *satori*, in which the seeker hovers for a moment on that razor's edge of form and formlessness, the soul who has dissolved into God reemerges with a vibrant wakefulness.

Teresa conceives of this experience as a living realization of the three divine Persons. The Father, the Son, and the Holy Spirit reveal themselves simultaneously to the soul in this moment. "Through a wondrous kind of knowledge," Teresa writes, "the soul apprehends the truth that all three divine Persons are one substance and one power and one knowing and one God alone."

In every room of the interior castle Teresa is there, reminding the seeker not to rest in a false sense of personal accomplishment but to remember always to praise God and love each other. Like Buddhism's *bodhisattva*, who arrives at the brink of liberation and then vows to return to the wheel of births and rebirths until all sentient beings are free, the soul who achieves union with God in the innermost chamber of the interior castle must return to the everyday world to be of service to other souls on the path. Far from rendering her incapable of performing ordinary tasks, the soul's experience of transformation in love creates an unshakable sanctuary of peace inside of her so that no matter what challenges life in the world may present, she can weather them joyfully, knowing that her Beloved dwells inside her and that he will never, ever leave her.

PROLOGUE

Few tasks that I have been commanded by obedience to undertake have been as difficult as this one. How do I write about matters of prayer? God has blessed me with neither the spiritual skillfulness nor the desire for it. Plus, for the past three months I have been suffering from such a clattering and fragility in my head that I have a hard time even focusing on mundane business matters.

But I have found that whenever I have surrendered in obedience, impossible things have become simple. While my physical nature rebels against the very prospect of a new book, I willingly take it on. I must admit, though, I cannot see how the Beloved thinks I will pull this off. He has not made me strong enough to prevent me from trembling with aversion when I am confronted with this continuous stream of health problems along with a multitude of demanding duties.

May he who has helped me with even more difficult things than this one help me now. Into his mercy I deliver my trust.

The truth is, I do not think I have much to say that I have not already said in other books I have been commanded to write. In fact, I am afraid I will just repeat myself. I feel like one of those birds they teach to speak who knows nothing except what it hears and then proceeds to repeat those things over and over again. If the Beloved wants me to say something new, he will reveal it to me. Otherwise, he will be pleased to help me remember things I have said in the past. My memory is getting so poor that I would be thrilled if I could recapture a few of the thoughts people have considered to be well said in the past so that they are not lost. Even if I do not remember a thing and I just get exhausted and my head hurts worse—even if no one finds anything I say to be of any use—I will be better for having surrendered in obedience.

And so today, on this feast day of the most blessed Trinity, in the year 1577, in this Carmelite convent of Saint Joseph's in Toledo, I begin to fulfill my agreement. In all that I say I submit to the wise ones who ordered me to write this. If I happen to say something that is not in alignment with what the Mother Church holds sacred, you can be sure that it will be through ignorance and not through malice. Know that by the goodness of God I ever am, have been, and shall be loyal to her. May God be forever blessed and glorified. Amen!

The man who ordered me to write this has suggested that the nuns in these convents of Our Lady of Mount Carmel could use a little assistance with certain questions they have about prayer. It seemed to him that women best understand the language spoken between women. He also thought that in light of their love for me, these nuns might pay special attention to what I have to say to them.

So it's important that I try to come up with something here and that I express it directly and clearly. It is ridiculous, of course, to think that what I would say could be of use to anyone else. But if these words inspire even one of my friends to praise God a little more, he will be granting me a great boon. The Beloved knows I am not interested in anything else. If I do manage to say something clearly, they will understand that it does not come from me. If they are mistaken about this it will be because they are as ignorant as I am inept. Only God in his mercy gives such things to us.

First Dwelling

Today while I was beseeching the Beloved to speak through me (since I couldn't think of anything to say and had no idea how to begin to fulfill this particular vow of obedience), I had a vision that I will share with you now as a foundation we can build on.

It came to me that the soul is like a castle made exclusively of diamond or some other very clear crystal. In this castle are a multitude of dwellings, just as in heaven there are many mansions.

If we muse on this deeply, friends, we will see that the soul of a righteous person is none other than a garden in which the Beloved takes great delight. What do you think a place might be like that such a king—so powerful and wise, so pure and filled with all good things—would find so delightful? I myself can come up with nothing as magnificent as the beauty and amplitude of a soul.

Our intellects, no matter how sharp, can no more grasp this than they can comprehend God. It is said, though, that he created us in his own image. If this is true (which it is), there is no point wearing ourselves out trying to fathom the great beauty of this castle with our mere minds. Even though the castle is a created thing, there is a vast difference between Creator and creature, so the fact that the soul is made in God's image means that it is impossible for us to understand her sublime dignity and loveliness.

What a shame that, through our own unconsciousness, we do not know ourselves! Wouldn't a person look foolish, friends, if you asked him who he was and he didn't know, had no idea who his father or mother were or what country he came from? If this seems stupid to you, know that our own stupidity is incomparably greater when we do not strive to know who we are. What transcends the body? We have heard that we have souls, and our faith compels us to believe that it is true. But we rarely consider the soul's excellent qualities or who it is that dwells within her or how precious she really is. And so we don't bother to tend her beauty. All our attention is focused on the rough matrix of the diamond, the outer walls of the castle, which are none other than these bodies of ours.

Remember, this castle has many dwellings: some above, some below, others to either side. At the center is the most important dwelling of them all where the most secret things unfold between the soul and her Beloved.

Hold this castle comparison in your mind. Maybe God will let it reveal to you a glimpse of the many different blessings that, as far as I have understood, he is happy to give to souls. The truth is, the blessings are so abundant no one could understand them all, especially someone as dense as I am. If you simply know that these things are possible, it will be a great consolation when they happen to you. Even if they do not, it will console you simply to praise God's great goodness.

It doesn't do any harm to reflect on heavenly bounty and on the joy that blessed ones feel, does it? In fact, it inspires us to strive for those delights ourselves. Neither does it harm us to find out that in the very midst of our exile such a great God chooses to associate with such wretched worms like ourselves. Seeing this, how could we do anything but love him for his perfect compassion and boundless mercy?

I am convinced that anyone who is bothered by the notion that the Beloved would grant such favors in the midst of our exile must be severely lacking in humility and love of neighbor. How else could she possibly be unhappy when God bestows his gifts on one of our brothers or sisters? This blessing of another in no way precludes his blessing of the rest of us. His Majesty can bless whoever he wants! Sometimes God reveals some great thing just to manifest his glory.

Remember when the disciples asked Christ if the blind man was suffering from his own transgressions or those of his parents? He gave the man back his sight. God does not grant glimpses of his grandeur on the basis that the one receiving such a glimpse is holier than the ones who do not. He does it so that we can recognize his glory and praise its manifestation in his creation. That is what happened, for instance, with Saint Paul and the Magdalene.

You could say that these blessings seem to be impossible and that it's not nice to upset the weak with false hope. But there is less to lose when we risk the chance that the weak ones might not believe in such holy things than there is when we hold back what we know from those who would most benefit from God's gifts. These are the souls who would be delighted by such gifts and would be awakened to an even greater love of the One who bestows them, the One whose power and glory are so vast. Anyone who does not believe in these blessings will not experience them. God appreciates it when we do not put limits on his works. And so, friends, try to never doubt the Beloved, even if he does not lead you by this path.

How do we get into our beautiful, delightful castle, after all? It must seem like I am talking nonsense. If this castle is the soul, you obviously cannot enter it, because it is inside yourself. It would be absurd to suggest that someone go into a room she is already in! But remember, there are many different ways to "be" in a place. Many souls hang around the outer courtyard where the guards are. They are not interested in getting inside the castle. They have no idea of what lies within this precious place or who lives in there or how many rooms there are. You know how some books on prayer recommend that you enter within yourself? That's exactly what I'm talking about, here.

Not long ago a very wise man told me that souls who do not practice prayer are like people whose limbs are paralyzed. Even though they have hands and feet, they cannot command them. And so there are souls so caught up in worldly matters that there is no hope for their recovery; they seem to be incapable of entering within themselves. These are souls so used to dealing with the nasty creatures that inhabit the outer walls of the castle that they have become almost like them. Even though they are naturally endowed with the power to commune with the Beloved himself, there is no remedy for them. Unless these souls strive to heal their profound misery, they will be turned into pillars of salt, just like Lot's wife was changed when she looked back.

It seems to me that the entry door to this castle is prayer and meditation. I do not mean just silent contemplation. When vocal prayer is accompanied by genuine reflection, it counts as true prayer. But if someone prays without awareness of who she is talking to, what it is she is asking, who is doing the asking and who is being asked, I do not consider it prayer, no matter how much her lips are moving. Even if she cannot consistently sustain this awareness, it does not matter, as long as she is truly reflective some of the time. If she gets into the habit of addressing the Magnificent One as if he were her servant, never questioning the manner in which she is expressing herself, merely letting whatever pops into her head fall out of her mouth, spilling words she has learned by simple repetition, she is not praying.

Please, Beloved, let no lover of God pray this way! At least among you, my friends, I beg you not to speak to God like that. The practice we have cultivated around here of focusing on interior things is a good safeguard against falling into such beastly ways.

I do not have a lot to say to these broken souls. Unless the Beloved himself comes and commands them to rise up, as he did to the man who lay for thirty years beside the pool, they are in big trouble. I am reaching out to the souls who ultimately will enter the castle. Even if they are somewhat absorbed in the world, their intentions are good. Every once in a while they do try to put themselves in God's hands and reflect on who they are, even if they do not linger in their meditations.

During the course of a month, these souls might pray a few times, but their minds are full of a thousand things they are still attached to. Where their treasure lies, says Christ, there also goes their heart. Every once in a while, though, they break free from these things and realize that they are not going the right way to get to the castle's front door. At last, they arrive. They enter the first, lower rooms. But so many reptiles have slipped in with them that they cannot even see the beauty of the castle or find any solace in it. Still, they have done very well to have gotten in at all.

D o you understand what would happen to this beautiful shining castle, this pearl of the east, this tree of life planted in the living waters of life itself, if the soul were to fall into grave error? No darkness is deeper than this. No blackness is more opaque. Although the same sun that has given the soul all her brilliance and beauty still shines at her center, it is as if the soul herself is no longer there to experience it. The soul is innately as capable of sharing this divine light as a crystal is in reflecting the radiance of the sun.

Nothing much helps a soul in a state of grave error. Any good works she may try to do are fruitless; she will gain no glory through them. If virtue is true virtue, its source is God. A soul in grave error has separated herself from God, and so her deeds are worthless. After all, a person who has fallen into grave error is interested in pleasing the spirit of evil, not God. And so the poor soul becomes the essence of darkness itself.

I know a certain person to whom God wanted to demonstrate what happens when a soul falls into grave error. This same person now believes that if only people really understood this, they would go to great lengths to avoid such occasions. May you, friends, share in this person's ardent desire for understanding! May the Beloved give you, as he has given her, the urge to pray fervently for other souls who are in this state, who have become sheer darkness and whose deeds are just as dark.

All streams flowing forth from a clear spring are also clear. So it is with a soul in grace. Planted like a tree in the spring of life, her deeds delight both the human and the divine. If it were not for this spring sustaining the tree and keeping it from drying up, there would be no cool shade, no sweet fruit. If the soul purposely pulls up her roots from the source and plants herself where the waters are black and smelly, nothing but misery and filth will flow forth from her.

This fountainhead that shines like the sun from the center of the soul never loses its radiance. It is ever-present within the soul and nothing can diminish its beauty. But obviously, if we were to drape a black cloth over a crystal sitting in the sunshine, no matter how brightly the sun shines it will have no effect on the shrouded jewel.

Oh, souls set free by the blood of Christ! Learn to understand yourselves. Have compassion for yourselves. With self-awareness, how could you not strive to lift the black veil that darkens the crystal of your soul? If your life were to end right now, you would never again be given to enjoy this light. Oh, Jesus! It is so sad to see a soul separated from this light. What a wretched state the chambers of the castle have fallen into. How disturbed are the faculties of sense and reason that inhabit them: these are the servants of the place; they have grown blind and badly behaved. But if a tree is planted in the spirit of evil, what other kind of fruit could it possibly bear?

I once heard a wise man say that it was not the things that a soul in grave error did but rather what she did *not* do. May God in his mercy deliver us from such wickedness! Nothing in this life deserves the name "evil" but this, which carries everlasting negativity in its wake. We must live alert to unconsciousness, friends, and pray to God to protect us against it. If he does not guard our city, then all our work is in vain. We are vanity itself.

That woman I mentioned said that she received two blessings from the gift the Beloved gave her. One blessing was an intense reluctance to offend God. Having learned the perils of unconsciousness, she begged him endlessly not to let her fall. The other blessing was that she discovered a mirror for humility inside herself which reflected the truth that none of our good works has its source in ourselves but flow instead from the sacred spring where this tree that is the soul is planted and in the divine sun that gives warmth to everything we do. She said this because it became so clear to her that whenever she did anything good or observed a good thing done she immediately recalled the source and understood that without it we are powerless. And so she would begin to spontaneously praise God, and she never gave a second thought to herself.

If we come away with these two blessings, friends, then neither the time you have spent in reading this nor I in writing it will have been wasted. Men of learning seem to get theology without much effort. But we women need to take it all in slowly and muse on it. We need to feel it. And so, if it be God's will, perhaps a few metaphors will capture our attention and bring some understanding.

These inner teachings are so obscure to the mind! Someone with as little learning as I have will end up saying countless superfluous and even irrelevant things in order to make a single meaningful point. Please have patience with me, dear reader, as I must cultivate patience with myself in writing of things I know almost nothing about. Because, really, sometimes I grab pen and paper like an utter fool. I have no idea whatsoever how I am going to begin and what I am going to say.

I fully understand how important it is for me to do my best to try to impart something useful to you about the inner life. We are always hearing about what a good thing prayer is. And we seekers are obligated to engage in it for so many hours a day. But all we are told is what we ourselves are supposed to do. What about the work the Beloved does inside us? The supernatural work? Nobody explains that part. It will be comforting to ponder the celestial palace within ourselves as we explore and explain the path of prayer. So few mortals understand this sacred place, although many pass through it. The Beloved may have given me some clarity about certain things I have written about in the past, but there are other more difficult matters I have not really begun to understand until now. The trouble is that, because of my own limitations, I cannot get to these mysteries without first going over what is already well known.

Let's get back to the mansion of many dwellings. Don't picture these dwellings as arranged in a row, one after the other. Instead, turn your eyes to the center, which is the part of the palace where the king lives. Imagine a palmetto fruit. Layer upon layer must be peeled away to reach the tasty part in the middle. So it is with the interior castle. Many rooms surround the central chamber. Always visualize your soul as vast, spacious, and plentiful. This amplitude is impossible to exaggerate. The soul's capacity far transcends our imagining. The sun at the center of this place radiates to every part.

It is very important for any soul who practices prayer—whether a little or a lot—not to limit herself or hold herself back in a designated corner. Since God has given her such dignity, let her roam freely through all the dwellings: above, below, and to each side. She must not feel compelled to linger too long in any one place, unless, of course, it is the dwelling of self-knowledge. How necessary this abode is, even for those whom the Beloved has drawn into the same chamber where he himself abides. No matter how high a state the soul attains, she can never neglect knowing herself, even if she wanted to.

Humility is always busy working, like a bee making honey in its hive. Without humility, all is lost. Remember, though: the bee continually goes out to gather more nectar from the flowers. And so the soul must fly sometimes from knowledge of herself to reflect on the majesty and greatness of her God. Aloft, she will recognize her own lowliness more clearly than if she were to only ponder her own nature. Plus, she will be freer from the serpents that invade those first chambers of self-knowledge. Even though it is by the grace of God that the soul practices knowing herself, you can, as the saying goes, have too much of a good thing. Believe me, reflecting on the virtue of God will carry us to much greater heights than if we were to tie ourselves down to our own little land of misery.

I am not sure I have explained this well. Self-knowledge is so important that I do not care how high you are raised up to the heavens, I never want you to cease cultivating it. As long as we are on this earth, there is nothing more essential than humility. Enter the room of self-knowledge first, instead of floating off to the other places. This is the path. Traveling along a safe and level road, who needs wings to fly? Let's make the best possible use of our feet first and learn to know ourselves. And yet it seems to me that we will never know ourselves unless we seek to know God. Glimpsing his greatness, we recognize our own powerlessness; gazing upon his purity, we notice where we are impure; pondering his humility, we see how far from humble we are.

What do we gain by this shift in perspective? A couple of things. First, it is clear that white seems much brighter against black and the black appears much darker set against the white. Also, when we turn away from our small selves and toward God, both our understanding and our will become more sublime and more inclined to embrace all that is good. We would do ourselves a great disservice if we never endeavored to rise above the mud of our personalized misery. Remember how dark and noxious are the streams that flow from the soul in grave error? It's a little bit like that. If we are perpetually stuck in our own acre of tribulation, our stream will never flow free from the mire of fear and faintheartedness.

Are they looking at me or not? we would be wondering. Will everything go wrong for me if I take this path? What's a wretched little person like me doing engaging in something as lofty as prayer? Won't I be perceived as superior if I don't follow the road everyone else is on? Extremes are no good, we would reason, even extremes in virtue. And, since I'm such a sinner, my fall would be even more catastrophic. Besides, I doubt I'd make any progress anyway, and I'm likely to just cause trouble to good people. Someone like me doesn't need to make herself into anything special.

Oh, God help me, friends! How many souls has the spirit of evil ruined in this way? They confuse these fears with humility. These fears arise from not knowing ourselves. Fear distorts knowledge of self. What we should really be afraid of is obsessing over ourselves and never getting free of ourselves! And so I say, my friends, let us set our eyes on Christ, our good, and on his saints. That is where we will learn true humility. Then our understanding will be enhanced. Then self-knowledge will not make us timid and cowardly.

Even though this is only the first dwelling of the interior castle, it is so rich and precious that the soul who can slip away from the serpents that slither in there cannot help but advance. The spirit of evil uses many nasty tricks to keep souls from knowing themselves and understanding their own paths!

I speak from experience when I warn you about this first dwelling. There aren't just a few rooms; there are millions. There are many ways for the soul, with all the best intentions, to get into trouble. But the intentions of the spirit of evil are always bad. And so in each room legions of evil spirits have been set up to beat back souls who try to pass from one room to the next. The poor souls who do not know about this fall for a thousand deceptions. The farther they travel away from the spirit of evil and the nearer they approach the innermost dwelling of the Beloved, the less likely they are to be tricked.

But souls in these first rooms are still attached to the world, still engulfed by their own pleasures and ambitions. The faculties of sense and reason, which God gave to the soul to be of service to her, may not be strong enough to combat certain forces. Some souls could be easily conquered here, even though they may do good works and be motivated by a sincere desire not to offend the Beloved.

Those who find themselves in this state should turn toward His Majesty as often as possible. They should call upon the Blessed Mother and all the saints to intercede on their behalf, since the servants of their own nature lack the power to defend them. The truth is, it is necessary at every single stage to draw what we need from God. May the Beloved in his mercy give us strength. Amen.

How miserable this life can be! I've gone on and on, here and elsewhere, about the ways we do damage to ourselves by failing to cultivate humility and self-awareness. Enough. Just remember: it is your most important task. Please God, may I have said something of benefit by now.

You will probably notice that the light from the king's innermost chambers seems to barely reach these first outer rooms. They are not black, as they are when the soul is darkened by a state of grave error, but the soul herself is prevented from seeing the light. Oh, I wish I knew how to explain myself! There is nothing wrong with this dwelling. It's just that those nasty creatures, like serpents and vipers and poisonous reptiles, creep into the soul and do not let her perceive the radiance. It is as if a person were to go into a room filled with sunshine but she had dirt in her eyes and could hardly open them. This dwelling is actually bright, but the soul cannot appreciate it because these wild beasts here make her close her eyes to everything but them.

It is not that the soul is in a wicked state. It is that she is still so immersed in the things of the world, still so caught up in possessions or honor or business affairs, that even though she may long to gaze upon the beauty of the interior castle, all these attachments distract her from doing so. She cannot seem to extricate herself from so many entanglements. But anyone who wishes to move ahead on the path must try to give up unnecessary objects and preoccupations. If you want to reach the innermost chamber, this is your only hope. Start now. Even if you have already entered the castle, you are still in danger. Among all those venomous creatures, you cannot avoid being bitten at some point.

What about people like us, friends, who have already freed ourselves from worldly attachments? What if we have already succeeded in entering deep into the secret dwellings within the castle of our souls and then, through our own fault, turn back toward chaos? Because of our imperfections, many of us who have been blessed by God fall back into a wretched state. We may live free from certain external involvements, but may God please grant us internal freedom as well! Guard yourselves, my friends, against matters beyond your control. Remember that evil spirits battle us throughout the kingdom. It is true that in some areas our faculties serve as our protectors and are strong enough to fight for our souls. But sometimes the spirit of evil disguises itself as an angel of light to deceive us. We cannot be too careful. If we do not remain conscious, the spirit of evil will sneak in and, like silent sandpaper, will gradually cause damage in all kinds of insidious little ways we may not even realize until it is too late.

For example, say the spirit of evil compels a certain sister to do endless penance. The only time she is at peace is when she is tormenting herself. Maybe the initial impulse toward self-mortification is pure, but it grows distorted. If her spiritual teacher has instructed that no one involve herself in those kinds of austerities without guidance but the sister believes she knows better and so engages secretly in such extremes anyway, compromising her health so that she becomes incapable of engaging in spiritual practice, then where has this seemingly good thing led her?

Maybe another sister suffers from a zeal for absolute perfection. Fundamentally this is a fine thing. But it could lead her to see every little fault in her friends as some serious transgression. She would be constantly on the lookout for other people's shortcomings and would be running to their spiritual guide to inform on them at every opportunity. This zeal could blind her to her own faults and alienate her friends who, resentful of her tendency to criticize, may not appreciate that it arose from a worthy impulse toward perfection.

Do not underestimate the spirit of evil, here. Its aim is to undermine charity and cool the love the friends have for one another. This would cause serious harm. Let's understand, my friends, that true perfection means loving God and loving our neighbor. The more perfectly we keep these two commandments, the closer to perfection we will come. All spiritual rules are nothing but means toward the end of spiritual love. Forget about reckless zeal. It can do harm. Let each one of us look to her self.

I do not want you to ever forget how important is the love between us. If you are going around looking at other people's faults, you might mistake insignificant things for drastic imperfections. This not only ruins your own serenity but unnecessarily disturbs other people's peace of mind. Perfection at what price?

The spirit of evil might even tempt our spiritual guides, which is all the more dangerous. Such a situation requires discretion. If the teacher herself breaks important spiritual rules, the kindest thing would be to call upon someone of higher station and prevail upon them to gently intervene. The same is true for one of the friends. Failing to deal with a problem out of fear of yielding to a negative temptation may be in itself yielding to a negative temptation. Still, it is important to remember that the spirit of evil has all kinds of tricks to deceive us; cultivating the habit of gossip is one of them. Don't talk about each other's faults behind each other's backs. For the greatest benefit, discuss these matters face to face. Around here, glory be to God, we don't have much opportunity for harmful chatter since we keep almost continual silence. But it is good to stay conscious of this tendency.

Second Dwelling

Who are the souls that make it through to the second dwelling and what are they doing there? I realize that I've written about this at great length in other places, but because I can't remember a thing I've said, I'm sure I'll end up repeating a lot of it here. As long as I say it in some new way, I trust you won't mind too much, since most of us never get tired of the multitude of books that deal with matters of the soul.

The second dwelling is for those who have already begun to practice prayer and become aware that it's time to move on beyond the dwelling of entry. But they haven't quite developed the fortitude to avoid falling back into occasions for spiritual error. At least now they understand the danger they

are in! They will be striving to flee from serpents and poisonous creatures because they have a much clearer sense of how
good it is to leave these things behind. Their hope for entering more deeply into the castle is much greater, now.

But the rooms of the second dwelling are harder to navi-
gate. Souls in the first dwelling have the dubious advantage of
being both deaf and dumb. Since they can hear nothing anyway, their inability to speak doesn't bother them much. To be
able to hear but unable to say anything is torment. This
doesn't mean, of course, that we should yearn for deafness,
because it is a wonderful thing to be capable of receiving what
is being transmitted to us. These are the souls who hear the
Beloved when he calls. They are getting closer to the place
where His Majesty dwells, and he is becoming a good neighbor to them.

We tend to get lost in our worldly affairs: buying and
selling, grasping and indulging, falling into spiritual error and
rising up again. These kinds of spiritual serpents are so viru-
lent and venomous, so numerous and dangerous, it would be
a miracle if we could avoid stumbling over them and falling.
Still, this Beloved of ours is merciful and good. Besides, he so
deeply longs for our love that he keeps calling us to come
closer. This voice of his is so sweet that the poor soul falls
apart in the face of her own inability to instantly do whatever
he asks of her. And so you can see, hearing him hurts much
more than not being able to hear him.

I am not saying that God calls to us directly, here, as he
will do later. For now, his voice reaches us through words spo-

ken by good people, through listening to spiritual talks, and reading sacred literature. God calls to us in countless little ways all the time. Through illnesses and suffering and through sorrow he calls to us. Through a truth glimpsed fleetingly in a state of prayer he calls to us. No matter how halfhearted such insights may be, God rejoices whenever we learn what he is trying to teach us.

Don't underestimate this first favor, friends, or be overly saddened if you cannot respond instantaneously to the call of the Beloved. His Majesty has no trouble waiting for many days, even years, especially when he sees that we are persevering and that our desires are good. Perseverance brings great gains.

But the spirit of evil assaults the soul in a thousand ways now and her suffering is deeper than it was before. In the first dwelling she could hear almost nothing, and she resisted less. She was a warrior who had lost hope of victory. The intellect has sharpened now and the faculties have grown more skillful. The clash of arms and the explosion of mortar are so intense that the soul cannot help but perceive them. Now the little demons present these serpents—which are worldly attachments and earthly pleasures—as if they were abiding realities. They suggest to the soul that in the world she is appreciated, that her friends and relatives are fond of her, that her impulse toward self-mortification is uncomfortable and unhealthy, and raise a thousand other theoretical impediments.

Oh, Jesus! What an uproar the spirits of evil create here!

The poor soul is afflicted by such confusion: should she push on or go back to the first dwelling?

When the soul compares all those worldly things to that which she is seeking, reason suggests that they may not be altogether worthless. But faith teaches the soul exactly what will make her whole. Memory demonstrates the impermanence of worldly things, reminding her of the deaths of people who used to take great pleasure in them. Some of these people died suddenly and were quickly forgotten. Some who enjoyed prosperity are now under the ground. She can reflect on their corpses being consumed by worms. The will, after seeing countless signs of love, inclines the soul to love in return. The will shows the soul that this is a Lover who will never leave her, that he walks with her always, giving her life and being. The intellect steps in to help the soul understand that she can never hope to have a better friend as long as she lives. It shows the soul that the world is filled with illusion and that these pleasures that the spirit of evil is dangling before her come laden with trials and tribulations, with worries and contradictions. It points out that she will find neither security nor peace outside the castle. The soul has no need to go off visiting strange houses since her own is brimming with blessings; all she has to do is enjoy them. Who is it that has everything she needs in her own house, whose guest lays out all good things at her feet? All the soul has to do is to cultivate the intention not to go astray like the prodigal son, who chose the food of swine.

Oh, my Lord and my God! This worldly habit of falling into vanities ruins everything. Our faith is so feeble that we desire what we can see rather than what faith is trying to tell us about. But when we take a good look, all we see is that those who pursue these visible vanities end up in nothing but misfortune.

It is the poisonous creatures we have been dealing with that cause all this trouble. When a viper bites someone and the wound swells, his whole being is toxified. If we do not take care of ourselves, this is what will happen to us. Many remedies will be required to cure us and only God's great mercy will keep our wound from killing us. Once the spirit of evil begins to detect that the character and habits of the soul indicate her readiness to move ahead on her path, all the powers of hell will be gathered to drive her back outside.

Oh, my Beloved! Here is where we need your help; without it we can do nothing. In your mercy, do not allow such a soul to suffer delusion and go astray when she has only just begun her journey. Give her light so that she may see that all goodness lies within and so that she may turn away from bad companions. It is a wonderful thing for the soul to connect with others who walk the way she is walking, who are not only sitting in the rooms she enters but who she knows have already ventured more deeply toward the center. Conversations with these travelers will be of great benefit to the soul; she can get close enough to them so that they will be able to take her with them.

May the soul always cultivate her intention not to be vanquished. If the spirit of evil sees that she is willing to lose her life, her tranquility, and everything else that it can offer rather than return to the first dwelling, it will soon give up on her. Let the soul be strong and not behave like those soldiers who knelt down to drink before going into battle. Let her be steadfast as she goes forth to stand against all the minions of unconsciousness raging inside her, knowing that there are no weapons superior to the peace of the cross.

If the soul were to be thinking about personal gratification at this stage, it would be a shaky way to build such a great and precious edifice of prayer. When a foundation is made on sand, the whole structure comes tumbling down. Souls seeking consolation will never be free of dissatisfaction and temptation. This is not the dwelling where manna rains from Paradise; that comes later, when a soul grows to want what God wants and finds in the manna all that her heart desires.

How strange! We still have a thousand imperfections and impediments. Our virtues are so young they have barely begun to grow. Thank God they have even been born! And yet we shamelessly grasp for spiritual satisfaction and complain about spiritual aridity. Please don't be like this, friends. Embrace the cross that your Beloved bore on his shoulders and accept that it is yours also to carry. Let she who is capable of the most intense suffering suffer most intensely for him; her liberation will be all the more perfect. If God grants you some sweet favor, give heartfelt thanks: this is purely a bonus.

It's tempting to think that if God would only grant you

internal favors you would be able to withstand external challenges. His Majesty knows what is best for us. He does not require our opinion on the matter and, in fact, has every right to point out that we don't have any idea what we're asking for. Remember: all you have to do as you begin to cultivate the practice of prayer is to prepare yourself with sincere effort and intent to bring your will into harmony with the will of God. I promise you that this is the highest perfection to be attained on the spiritual path. The more perfectly you practice this surrender, the greater the gifts you will receive from the Beloved and the farther you will advance on your journey.

Don't think you have to use esoteric jargon or dabble in the mysteries of the unknown. If we miss the mark right at the beginning, trying to direct things according to our own cravings in hopes that God will cooperate, what kind of base are we laying down for our sacred edifice? Let's do whatever we can to avoid those poisonous little reptiles. Sometimes it is actually God's will that we are plagued by bad thoughts we cannot get rid of and spiritual aridity we cannot alleviate. Sometimes he even lets the serpents bite us to see if we suffer grief for having offended him and so that we learn to guard ourselves better against future error.

And if you fall sometimes, do not lose heart. Keep striving to walk your path with integrity. God will draw out the good even from your fall, just as the man who sells antidotes will drink poison to test their effectiveness. If nothing else could highlight our own misery or reveal to us the harm we are doing to ourselves by living a dissipated life, this battle unfolding inside of us would be enough to bring us back to recollection. What could be worse than not being at home in our own house? What hope do we have of finding rest outside of ourselves if we cannot be at ease within? Whether or not we appreciate them, we must always live in close proximity to our faculties: they are our greatest relatives and most faithful friends. And yet, as if they were resentful of the damage our imperfections have done to them, our faculties seem to be waging war upon us.

Peace, peace, Christ says, my friends. He often urged peace upon his own disciples. Believe me, if we don't cultivate peace at home, we will not find it in alien places. End the war! By the blood that he shed for us, I ask those of you who have not begun to go inside yourselves to enter now, and those who are already in: don't let warfare make you turn back. A relapse is worse than a lapse; you can already see what you've lost. Trust more in the mercy of God and less in your own judgment. Then you will see how His Majesty brings you safely from one dwelling to the next and settles you in a land where those wild beasts cannot touch you or do you any harm. You yourself will have power over these creatures; you will laugh at them. You will enjoy more blessings than you ever imagined—in this life, I mean.

Remember: when you are tormented by the spirit of evil, you cannot recollect yourself by force. Recollection must come gently. Little by little you will be able to practice prayer for longer periods undisturbed. Don't neglect to consult people with experience so that they can assure you there is nothing wrong with your practice, that you are doing exactly what you are supposed to be doing. Even if you encounter no one to teach you, don't give up. The Beloved will guide you on your path. There is no other remedy for the error of quitting your practice except to start up again at the beginning. Otherwise, the soul loses more of herself every day. May it please God, my friends, that you come to understand how this works.

Some of you may think that if turning back is so bad it would be better never to have begun, that you might as well have stayed outside the castle in the first place. I told you right from the start—and Christ himself has said—that whoever walks in danger shall perish in it. The door to this castle is prayer. It is ridiculous to think that we can enter Paradise without first entering ourselves! We must get to know ourselves, reflect on our limitations, acknowledge our gratitude for God, and solicit his mercy.

Christ, who is love, says: No one gets to the Father except through me (or something like that). He also says: He who sees me sees my Father. Well, if we never look at him or reflect on what he has given us and the death that he endured for us, then I can't imagine how we will come to know him or do good works in service of him. What is faith worth without works? What are works worth without connection to the goodness of Christ? Who will awaken us to love this Beloved?

May His Majesty give us understanding of the magnitude of his sacrifice, reminding us that the servant is not greater than the master and that we need to exert effort to harvest his glory.

And so we must pray without ceasing and leave temptation behind.

Third Dwelling

B lessed are those in awe of God."
What else can we say of one who has persevered, has transcended all those conflicts, and entered safely into the third dwelling?

It is no small task for His Majesty to help me understand the living poetry of this verse since I get very confused about these matters. Of course such a one is blessed! Unless she turns back, she is on the straight path to liberation. Can you see, friends, how important it is to have overcome the battles of the past? I am convinced that the Beloved never fails to bless these triumphant souls with a secure conscience. I said secure, but I was mistaken. There is no security in this life.

Whenever I use a term like that, just translate it as: "unless she abandons the path she set out on."

It is such a burden to be alive when we have to walk around like men with enemies at their threshold. These warriors can't eat or sleep unless their weapons are within easy reach. They live in perpetual fear that their adversaries might discover a weak spot in their fortress and break through with a surprise attack.

Oh, my Beloved, my greatest good! Why would you want us to want such a miserable existence? It is impossible for us to stop begging you to take us out of it. Our only hope is in losing ourselves in you, in spending this life absorbed only in serving you, and in trying to understand your will in keeping us here. If it is your will, my God, let us die with you, as Saint Thomas says. Living without you is nothing but dying over and over again. Living without you is nothing but living in dread of the possibility of losing you forever.

And so I say, friends, the blessedness we ask for should be the security of knowing that we are already blessed. What pleasure can anyone have, whose sole pleasure is in serving God, when she is plagued by such fears? Remember, there are some saints who enjoyed heightened states beyond measure and still fell into grave error. We can never be sure that God will reach out his hand and pull us up from unconsciousness.

I have to admit to you, my friends, I am so terrified as I write this that I don't know how I'm writing it or how I live when I even think about it, which I do constantly. Please pray, my friends, that His Majesty be with me always. Otherwise, what hope can there be for a life as poorly spent as mine? Don't be sad when I say this, as I have seen you get before. I know that you would like to believe that I have lived a purely holy life, and it depresses you to hear that it might not be so. I don't blame you. Believe me, I wish myself that I had maintained such a high level of holiness.

But what can I do? Whatever I've lost has been lost through my own fault. I refuse to complain about a God who has given me everything I need to be the way you wish I really were. I cannot say this without crying. How confusing! Who am I to be writing something to those who could just as well be teaching me? This has been such a difficult order to obey! But, since I am doing this for the sake of the Beloved, may it be of some benefit to you. Perhaps you could ask him to pardon this brazen woman. His Majesty knows well that the only thing I can count on is his mercy. Since I cannot un-be what I have been, all I can do is take refuge in his compassion and trust in the excellence of his son and of the Virgin, his mother, whose robes both you and I wear.

Praise her, my friends! You truly belong to the mother. And when you have such a good mother, you have no reason to be ashamed of my imperfections. Emulate her. Reflect on how great Our Lady really is. Acknowledge how blessed we are to have her as our advocate. Even my being what I am, with all my errors and unconsciousness, is not enough to tarnish our sacred sisterhood in the slightest.

But I have to warn you about one thing: just because you have a mother like ours, don't be too sure of yourselves. Look how holy David was. And you know what became of Solomon. Don't put too much stake in the fact that you have withdrawn from the world and that spiritual practice is a way of life for you. Do you think you're safe because you are in continual conversation with God and practice prayer day and night? All of this is very good, but it is not sufficient reason to cease being in awe of God. Continue repeating this prayer and hold it close to your heart: *Beatus vir, qui timet Dominum* [Psalm III:1].

What a lengthy digression! Now I've forgotten what I was talking about. Whenever I think about myself I feel so helpless, like a bird with a broken wing. I'm not sure I'm sharing anything of value here, so I think I'll leave all that behind for now and get back to what I was saying about the souls who have made their way to the third dwelling.

The Beloved has shown these souls immense mercy in seeing them through their initial difficulties. I believe that, through the goodness of God, there are many souls like these in this world. They are so reluctant to offend His Majesty that they carefully avoid even petty imperfections. They use their time wisely, spending long hours in meditation. They practice acts of compassion toward their neighbor and are balanced in their speech and appearance. If they have a household, they manage it harmoniously. This is certainly the behavior to be cultivated for those who wish to enter the ultimate dwelling, and I don't see any reason why the Beloved should deny any favor to those who truly yearn to be with him.

Oh, Jesus! Who could ever suggest that these souls, having endured such strife to arrive at this place, are not motivated by a one-pointed desire for absolute goodness? No one! We all go around saying that this is what we want, but words are not enough. We need more than speech if the Beloved is going to take up full possession of our souls.

Remember the young man who was told by the Beloved exactly what he had to do if he wished for perfection? Ever since I first began to speak of these dwellings, I have had this youth in mind because he is just like us. This is where those long periods of aridity and doubt come from. I'm not talking about the inner trials that some poor seekers go through, like general depression and other kinds of soul-sickness. Those are states that can be truly unbearable, and they are no fault of the seeker. The Beloved will eventually rescue them from this kind of suffering; we have to let God be the judge of such things. I'm referring to souls who would never commit even a minor error intentionally. They live with integrity. They consider themselves to be God's devoted servants, and so they cannot just patiently accept it when they find the door to the king's chamber closed. But even on this earth a ruler might have many servants and not all of them get to enter his sanctum.

Go in, go in, my friends! Enter the innermost rooms of your selves. Move on from your small works. Through your love of Christ you can do so much more than that. You should be content to simply be God's servants. If you want too much, you might end up with nothing. Look at those holy ones who have successfully entered the chamber of God and you will see the difference between them and us. Don't ask for what you haven't earned. No matter how much we may have served God, we have also let him down. It's foolhardy to walk around thinking we have any kind of special entitlement.

Oh, humility, humility! I'm not sure what kind of subtle temptation I might be succumbing to here, but I can't seem to resist judging those who make such a big deal about periods of aridity as being somewhat lacking in humility. Let us test ourselves, my friends, or let the Beloved test us. He knows exactly how to do it, even if we don't want to understand him.

Let's take another look at the souls of the third dwelling who have cultivated harmonious lives. Notice all they do for God. What right do we have to complain? There's God, telling us what we need to do to achieve perfection, and there we are (like that young man in the gospel), turning our backs on him and walking away sad. What do we expect His Majesty to do about that? Isn't the love he offers us proportionate to the love we bear him? This is not a love, my friends, that is manufactured in the imagination; it is proved by action. Still, don't assume that God has any need for our doing. What he needs is our being. He needs the clear intent of our will.

We seem to think that when we withdraw from worldly ways, take on the mantle of renunciation, and forfeit per-

sonal power and possessions for the sake of the Beloved, we
have given all that we can give. Although the things we relin-
quished may not add up to much, they are all we have, and so
it feels like a huge sacrifice. This is an excellent beginning. As
long as we persevere and don't go back—as long as we don't
even desire to go back—to dance with the serpents in the
first rooms, we will attain our goal. We must strip ourselves
naked and cultivate detachment from the things of the world.

But I warn you: abandon yourselves only under the condition that you harbor no illusions about the Beloved being
under some obligation to repay you for your sacrifice with
divine favors. It was either Saint Paul or Christ who reminded
us that we are simply servants of our God. The more you
receive, the deeper should be your gratitude. What can we
offer such a generous Beloved, who died for us and breathes
life into our being? Shouldn't we consider ourselves blessed
to have the chance to repay even a fraction of what we owe
him for the ways in which he has served us? I use this term
"service" with some trepidation, but it's true: during all the
time he walked this world, he did nothing but serve. Do we
have to keep asking him for more gifts, more favors?

I know that I have presented all this in a jumble, friends,
but I'm not sure how else to explain it. Reflect deeply on
these things and the Beloved will make them clear. Then,
periods of aridity will make you humble instead of ill at ease.
Be assured that where there is humility, God will grant the
peace that comes from being aligned with his will. If you do
not receive specific consolations, remember that this inner

tranquility yields a deeper contentment. His Divine Majesty gives consolations to the weaker souls among us who would not willingly exchange these tokens for the fortitude earned by those who dare to walk through the desert of the soul. We are more attracted to sweetness than we are to the cross.

Test us, Beloved, you who know the truth, so that we may know ourselves.

. 2 .

I have known quite a few souls who have lived for a number of years in a righteous and orderly way, both physically and spiritually. Then, after all that time, when it seems that they have become masters of this world, or at least radically detached from it, His Majesty sends them a few small tests and they react far out of proportion to the challenges they face. They mope around so disturbed and distressed it bewilders and even frightens me. It's no use offering them advice. They have been engaged in spiritual practice so long they think they should be teaching others and that they are perfectly justified in feeling the way they do.

I haven't found any way to comfort or cure these people. All I can do is express compassion for their trouble which, when I see them so miserable, rises spontaneously from my heart. Why try to contradict their reasoning? They have convinced themselves that they are suffering for God's sake, and it never enters their mind that they might be suffering as a result of their own shortcomings.

This is another mistake some advanced souls make. They shouldn't be so surprised by their own suffering. Sometimes it is God's will that his loved ones become conscious of their limitations, and so he withdraws his support a little. Not much of this kind of pain should be required for them to quickly come to know themselves. They would clearly recognize their own imperfections and immediately understand what is happening to them. They would realize that they are overly attached to unimportant worldly matters, and then this imperfection of theirs would cause them more pain than whatever it was that was troubling them to begin with. This kind of distress is, I believe, a great mercy from God. Even though it compels them to painfully confront their own flaws, they grow in humility.

But for the unconscious people I am talking about, it's not like that. They glorify their tribulations in their own minds and would like everybody else to exalt them. I want to say a little something about these things so that we can understand and test ourselves before the Beloved tests us. It's a great advantage to be able to prepare with self-knowledge ahead of time.

Say there is a wealthy person who has no family and he loses his fortune. He still has enough to take care of his necessities and even a bit left over. If he becomes as anxious and worried as if he didn't even have a crust of bread to eat, how can our Beloved ask him to leave everything behind for his sake? Maybe he will claim that he is so upset because he wanted to give that money to the poor. But I believe that God would rather have me align with the divine will and maintain the tranquility of my soul than fret over my own agenda for charity. If the Beloved has not yet led the rich man far enough that he can attain this peace, that's fine. All he needs to do is to understand that he is lacking freedom of spirit and he should ask the Beloved for it. His Majesty is going to require it later, so he should be ready.

Say there is another person who has more than enough to meet his needs and is faced with the opportunity for acquiring more property. Well, congratulations, go right ahead. But what if he strives for wealth and after obtaining it strives for more and more? If his intentions are good and he has cultivated virtue through spiritual practice, he doesn't have to be so afraid of reaching the dwelling closest to the king.

A similar thing happens when such people are confronted with an occasion for being misunderstood or losing a bit of their reputation. God will usually grant them the grace to handle this skillfully. He is fond of favoring virtue in public so that virtue itself will not suffer. Maybe he helps them because they have served him. This Beloved of ours is very good! Still, they are plunged into disquiet because they cannot instantaneously conquer the distress that rises in their hearts.

God help me! Aren't these the same people who not very long ago were musing on how the Beloved suffered and what a noble thing it is to suffer and have even desired suffering for themselves? They wish everyone would live as orderly a life as theirs. All we can hope is that they will not presume that their pain is a response to other people's faults and convert it in their minds to something lofty.

Maybe you think, friends, that I am wandering off the subject or that these examples have nothing to do with us since these are not issues that arise around here. We have no wealth, nor do we strive for any, and nobody is trying to undermine anybody else's worldly status. But we can learn many lessons from comparisons. There's no need for me to elaborate. The purpose of these analogies is for you to consider if you have truly detached yourself from that which you have given up. Little things arise all the time that can serve to test you and prove if you have achieved mastery over your own cravings. Believe me, this has nothing to do with whether or not you wear religious robes. It's a matter of practicing the virtues, of surrendering to God in everything, of bringing our lives into harmony with whatever His Majesty arranges for us, of desiring that his will—not ours—be done. Maybe we have not yet evolved this far. Humility, I say! Humility is the ointment for our wounds. If we are truly humble, then God, the great physician, will eventually come to heal us.

Whenever these souls practice renunciation, they do it in the same well-balanced manner with which they order their lives. They have an intense thirst for self-sacrifice as a means of serving God. There is nothing wrong with this. They tend to be discreet in their ascetic practices, careful not to compromise their health. They are reasonable people, in no danger of killing themselves with austerities. Their love is not yet powerful enough to overwhelm their reason.

Oh, if only our love would make us dissatisfied with this modest little way of serving God: with timid baby steps. We'll never reach the end of our journey at this pace! It may seem to us as if we were endlessly walking and we're getting tired. Believe me, it is an exhausting journey. Sometimes it may feel like enough simply to avoid going astray.

But if we could travel from one realm to another in eight days, friends, would it be a wise thing to take a year to get there, through snow and rain and bad roads? Wouldn't it be better to get the journey over with as quickly as possible? All these obstacles do arise, plus the danger of serpents. Oh, could I give you some good examples of these! Please God that I may have passed beyond this stage myself. Often enough it seems to me that I haven't.

When we are hyper-vigilant, we fear everything and everything offends us. We don't dare to move forward, as if we could reach the ultimate dwelling by leaving it to others to make the journey for us. Since that is impossible, why don't we exert ourselves, my friends, for love of our Beloved? Let's abandon our reason and fear into his hands. Forget about the weakness in our nature that we worry about so much. Let our families look after the safekeeping of our physical form; that's their concern. All we should focus on is getting to see this Beloved of ours as soon as possible.

Even if there is not much comfort on this path, we would be making a big mistake to fret about our health. Anxiety over our health does not improve it one bit; this I know. I also know that this entire business has very little to do with the body, which is the least important part. The journey I'm talking about requires great humility. If you have understood things so far, you will see that it is lack of humility that has prevented you from making progress in the past. It may seem that we have advanced only a few small steps while our friends have made vast strides. Believe this. Let us acknowledge our own limitations and pray for the success of others.

If we practice humility, this stage is a most excellent one. If not, we may waste our whole lives here, suffering a thousand miseries. Unless we abandon ourselves, this state is arduous and burdensome. We would be trudging under the load of our egos, like mud clinging to our boots and dragging us down. Those who reach the ultimate dwelling bear no such baggage.

Still, even in these rooms, the Beloved never fails to reward us with greater spiritual sweetness than we could ever glean from the distractions and satisfactions of mundane life. He is infinitely merciful and always gives us more than we have earned. But he bestows these blessings sparingly, inviting us to catch glimpses of what is unfolding in the dwellings ahead so that we can prepare ourselves for entering them.

It may sound like spiritual sweetness and consolation are

the same thing. Why do I make this distinction? I could be wrong, but I think there's a great difference between them. There will be more to say about this when we come to the fourth dwelling. That's when I will describe the profound spiritual delights the Beloved gives us. And yet, although such a discourse might appear to be pointless at this juncture, it could be somewhat helpful to explore the nature of each so that you can distinguish between sacred sweetness and ordinary gratification and strive to choose the better one.

Great solace can come to souls whom God brings to the fourth dwelling. Those who thought they already knew everything will be confused, while humble souls will be moved to give thanks. The ones who lack some humility will taste an inner bitterness they cannot explain. Perfection isn't about consolation; it's about loving. We are rewarded by doing whatever we do with righteousness and love.

You may wonder if this is true. It is. Why bother discussing these interior mercies? I don't know. Ask the men who ordered me to write this. I am under an obligation to obey them and not dispute them.

All I can tell you is that there was a time when I did not know about these divine favors through experience or believe I would ever in my life be given to know them. That was fine with me. It gave me ample joy to know by simple inference that I must be pleasing to God in some way. When I read in books about the tender mercies and spiritual sweetness God grants souls who serve him, it comforted me and moved me to passionately praise him.

Well, if my soul, which was so undeveloped, responded like this, think of how much greater will be the praise offered to God by those of you who are humble and good. If even one soul is inspired to praise him, I think it's worth bringing up the subject. We need to become aware of the sweetness and delight we forfeit through our own imperfection. When these favors come from God, they come overflowing with love, infusing the soul with the fortitude she needs to make her journey less laborious and to help her grow in spiritual practice and in virtue. Don't think that our participation in this doesn't count. When we cultivate consciousness, we can be sure the Beloved will be just. If we are denied the consolations we crave, he will bless us in another way. His secrets are deeply hidden. But without a doubt, whatever he does will be exactly the right thing for us.

For those who are in this state, I would suggest that you learn to be responsive to the divine will. Remember, it is by the goodness of God that you have come this far. He is granting you no small mercy when he brings you to this place because this means he is about to take you higher. Surrender. Even if you are not part of a formal spiritual community, it would be great if you had someone to go to who would make sure you were not following your own will in anything. Most of us do have such a person in our lives. It is in doing what we want that we usually get into trouble. But don't pick anyone who is just like you, nervous about every little thing. Seek out someone who is free from illusion about the world. It is very important to consult with those who see things as they really are if we want to come to know ourselves. Plus, it's encouraging to encounter a soul who easily achieves what has felt impossible to us. By observing their flight, we might dare to fly. We are like fledgling birds who may not be ready to immediately soar but, by watching the parents, little by little learn to emulate them. This kind of assistance, I know, is a great advantage.

Still, no matter how determined such souls are not to dishonor God, it's a good idea to avoid taking any chances. Since they are not far from the first dwelling, it would be easy to slip back there. Their fortitude is not built on solid ground, as it is for those whose foundation has been forged by suffering. Those who have suffered know firsthand about the storms of this region and are not afraid of them. They have no appetite for the consolations of the world. But if these young souls knew about the suffering, they might be tempted to escape to the false refuge of earthy gratification.

The spirit of evil knows just how to stir up tempests that will do us harm. While these souls might be forging ahead with great zeal, trying valiantly to keep others from falling into unconsciousness, they might be incapable of resisting their own temptations or withstanding their own tribulations.

Let's stop focusing on the imperfections of others and take a look at our own. Those who lead such orderly lives are easily shocked. We can learn important lessons from those who shock us, even if on the outside we are better behaved. Outward composure is fine, but it's not the most important thing. There is no reason to think that everyone else should follow our path. We shouldn't presume to lead other people onto the way of the spirit when we ourselves don't even know yet what that is.

With the urge God gives us to help others, friends, we can delude ourselves. It's better to concentrate our attention on what our tradition teaches: strive to live always in silence and hope. The Beloved will take care of his own. All we have to do is beseech His Majesty on their behalf and we will, with his help, be doing much good.

May he be forever blessed.

Fourth Dwelling

. I .

As we begin to explore the fourth dwelling, I pause to surrender myself again to the Holy Spirit. I pray that from this point onward he take over and speak for me so that you can most clearly hear what needs to be said about the remaining chambers in this castle of the soul.

Now is when we enter the realm of the supernatural. Fourteen years ago, when I wrote the *Book of My Life,* His Majesty explained these ineffable matters for me, and I'm counting on him to do it again here. Although I think I am a little more enlightened now about these mercies the Beloved grants to some souls, knowing how to describe them is a different thing. If there is any benefit in efforts to express the inexpressible, may His Majesty help me to do so now. If not, so be it.

Since these dwellings are getting nearer to where the king lives, they are more beautiful. There are things to see and understand here so sublime that unless someone had direct experience with them words would be useless to convey them and the mind incapable of grasping them. Someone with a great deal of spiritual background will understand the subtleties perfectly. Although generally a person must have lingered long in the previous dwellings before entering this one, there are no rules about that. The Beloved gives when he wishes, as he wishes, and to whom he wishes. Since these blessings come from him, of course, injustice is not possible.

Poisonous creatures rarely enter these dwellings. When they do, they are usually harmless and may even do the soul some good. In this stage of prayer, it is helpful to have some of them around launching a few battles in the soul. If there were no temptations, the spirit of evil could more easily slip in and deceive the soul about the spiritual delights she is being given by God. If she were not struggling with temptation, the soul would not be gaining merit. She would collapse into a state of habitual absorption, deprived of the opportunity to grow. I don't consider it safe to stay in such a state. I don't even think it's possible for the Spirit of the Lord to remain perpetually fixed in the soul during this life of exile.

What, then, is the difference between spiritual sweetness and consolations in prayer? It seems to me that we can be consoled through our own meditations and through our supplications to our Beloved. Although God does have a hand in them (as he does, of course, in everything), consolations spring from our own nature. What I mean is that solace arises from the virtuous acts we perform. It feels like we've earned it through our own efforts. It is correct for us to feel consoled when we act righteously.

But ponder this and you will see that we can derive the same kind of satisfaction from various worldly experiences, for instance: if we were to suddenly inherit an unanticipated fortune; if we met someone and fell madly in love when we weren't even looking for love; if we were to succeed in some significant business venture and everyone praised our skill; if we had been told that our husband or brother or daughter was dead and then they came back to us alive. I have seen people weep for pure joy. I have even done so myself.

I believe that the joyful feelings that come to us from God are similar to natural consolations, except that their source is nobler. This is not to suggest that worldly delights are in any way a bad thing. What I'm trying to say is that earthly satisfactions spring from our own nature and end in God; spiritual sweetness begins in God and makes its way into our human nature where we delight in it far more than we enjoy the worldly kind of gratification.

Oh, Jesus, how I long to be able to explain this! I clearly perceive an important distinction between these two states, and yet I do not have the skills to communicate it. May the Beloved do it for me.

I just remembered the verse we say at the end of the last

psalm at Prime: *Cum dilatasti cor meum*. For those who know from experience the difference between these things, no further explanation is necessary; for those who don't, more words are required.

Natural consolations do not expand the heart. Sometimes they even constrain it a little. The soul may feel profoundly happy when she thinks she is doing something for God. But sometimes she sheds bitter tears springing from the passions. I don't know that much about these passions of the soul. If I did, maybe I would be more successful in explaining which issue from the sensual part of our nature and which come from a higher place. I have been through this, but I am powerless to explain it. If only I could! Knowledge and learning can be such a great help in everything.

When I would experience this state of sweetness and spiritual blessing in prayer, if I began to weep over the Passion of Christ, I could not stop until my head was burning. If I wept over my imperfections, the same thing happened: copious tears and splitting headaches. The Beloved was doing me a big favor in this. Sometimes tears flow from moments like these and intense longings rise up. They are reinforced by human nature and by our individual personalities. They always come to rest in God. As long as there is humility and the soul understands that she is no more special than anyone else for having such experiences, these feelings are a great blessing. It's not possible to know whether or not they spring from pure love, but if they do, they belong to God alone.

It is mostly the souls in the first three dwellings who

apprehend feelings of devotion. These are the souls who apply the discursive mind to their meditations. This is all they have. It would be good for them to spend some time actively praising God, rejoicing in his goodness and in his being what he is, and desiring his honor and glory. They should do this as much as possible because such acts of love are great awakeners of the will. If the Beloved fills the soul with blessings like these, she should not turn away from them for the sake of completing her prescribed meditation.

Remember: if you want to make progress on the path and ascend to the places you have longed for, the important thing is not to think much but to love much, and so to do whatever best awakens you to love.

Maybe we don't know what love is. It wouldn't surprise me one bit to find out that this is true. That's because love is not about our own happiness but about trying to please God in every way. Loving God means striving not to dishonor him. Loving God means asking that the beauty of his Son be celebrated among the people. These are signs of love. Don't assume that you're never supposed to think about anything else and that if you become a little distracted all is lost.

I used to be tormented by this turmoil of thoughts. A little over four years ago I came to realize by experience that thinking is not the same as mindfulness. I asked a wise man about this and he affirmed my insight, which thrilled me. I hadn't been able to understand why, if the mind is one of the faculties of the soul, it is sometimes so restless. Thoughts fly around so fast that only God can anchor them, and when he does we feel almost as if we were disconnected from the body. It was driving me crazy to see the faculties of my soul calmly absorbed in remembrance of God while my thoughts, on the other hand, were wildly agitated.

Oh, Beloved, bear in mind what anguish we have to suffer on this path through lack of knowing the truth. The trouble is that since we think all we have to do is concentrate our thoughts on you, we can't even conceive of how to ask the ones who know the truth about this or comprehend how to frame the question in the first place. We suffer terrible trials because we do not understand ourselves. We worry about things that we think are bad but which are actually good things.

This lack of knowledge afflicts many people who practice prayer. They complain of interior trials, grow depressed, and their health declines. They may even abandon prayer altogether. These are people who have not learned to look inside themselves and discover the inner world there. Can we stop the stars from hurtling across the heavens? No. We cannot stop the mind, either. Off it goes, and then we send all the faculties after it. We end up thinking we are lost and blaming ourselves for wasting precious time in the presence of God.

But it could be that the soul is fully present with him in the innermost chamber while the mind stays on the periphery of the palace, grappling with a thousand wild and dangerous creatures and gaining real merit from this kind of struggle. The spirit of evil would like nothing better than for us to just give up at this point and abandon our spiritual practice. Don't lose heart. Trials and disturbances like these come mostly from not understanding ourselves.

As I write this, by the way, I can't help but wonder what's going on inside my own head. Those noises I told you about in the beginning are getting so loud that it's almost impossible for me to obey the order to write this. It sounds like there are a multitude of rushing rivers inside my head, their waters cascading downward, surrounded by many little birds and other whistling sounds. This is all unfolding not in the ears but in the upper part of the head, where they say the higher part of the soul resides. I have spent long periods in these regions. The spirit seems to push its way upward with great power and speed. Please God that I remember to mention the reason for this when we get to the later dwellings because this is not quite the right place to go into it. I would not be surprised to find out that the Beloved has given me this trouble in my head just so that I can understand all this better. The truth is, all this turmoil does not hinder my prayer or interfere with what I am trying to say. Instead, my soul is whole within its quietude, its love, its longing, and its clarity of consciousness.

But if the higher part of the soul is in the upper part of the head, why isn't the soul disturbed by all that commotion? I don't know about that. But I do know that what I've been saying is true. When prayer is not accompanied by the suspension of the faculties, it hurts. When the faculties are suspended, we do not feel pain until they are engaged again. It would be a travesty to let this problem convince us to give up on prayer. It isn't good to let our thoughts disturb us or worry us at all. If they come from the spirit of evil, they'll pass. But if this misery is part of our legacy from Adam's weakness and from our own imperfections, let us suffer it patiently for the love of God. After all, we put up with eating and sleeping and cannot avoid them, even though we might sometimes wish to.

Let us acknowledge our misery. Let us yearn for that place where no one can scorn us. I'm thinking of the words the bride sang in the Song of Songs, and I see that they apply perfectly here. It seems to me that none of the contempt or tribulation we endure in this life can compare to those inner battles. If we find peace where we live, there is no conflict that can disquiet us. But if the cause of our strife is within ourselves, then no matter how much we desire relief from the thousand trials of this world and no matter how much the Beloved desires this tranquility for us, the results will be almost unbearably painful. And so, Beloved, please raise us to the place where the miseries that taunt the soul relent. God will free the soul from suffering when he delivers her into the final dwelling, even in this very lifetime. If it be his will, we shall explore this.

These miseries do not torment everyone as badly as they afflicted me for so many years. I thought I had been a bad person, and it seems to me in retrospect that I was trying to get back at myself. Because the experience was so painful for me, I feel like I should share it in case it is like that for you, too. I will try describing it in a number of ways so that you will see that this kind of thing is unavoidable and should not overly disturb you. Just let that old mill go on clacking around and around and continue grinding your own flour. Don't let the will or the understanding stop working.

Depending on our health and on the effects of time, this trouble will be more intense or less so. Even if it is not the poor soul's fault, she will suffer anyway. We will commit other errors altogether, so we might as well practice patience. Although we are continually advised in our reading and counseling not to pay too much attention to our thoughts, we do not seem to quite get it. So I don't think it's a waste of time for me to go into it more deeply and try to offer you some comfort. Of course, until the Beloved chooses to enlighten you, these words won't help much. Still, I think that His Majesty wishes we would do whatever it takes to understand ourselves.

We need to quit blaming the soul for problems caused by a weak imagination, human nature, and the spirit of evil.

God help me in this mess I have gotten myself into! I have forgotten what I was writing about last. Business and health matters forced me to set the work aside just when we were getting up to the best part so far. Since I have such a poor memory, it will probably all be very confusing from here on because I simply cannot bear to go back and read it over again. This is what I'm worried about, anyway.

It seems to me that I was talking about consolations in prayer and how they are sometimes entwined with our passions. This can trigger fits of sobbing. I have heard some people say that they experience a sense of constriction in their chests and even uncontrollable movements in their limbs. These experiences can be so powerful that they cause nosebleeds and other painful effects. Since I haven't been through anything like this myself, I can't say much about it. I'm sure these kinds of things must be very consoling, though, because they're all about loving God and basking in his presence.

What I call spiritual sweetness is a very different thing. Those of you who have experienced this will know what I mean. In other books I have referred to this state as the Prayer of Quiet.

See if this image helps you understand what I mean. There are two fountains and they each have a basin to be filled with water. (You know, I haven't found any better metaphor for describing certain spiritual experiences than water. I love this element; I have spent a great deal of time contemplating it.) These two basins fill up in different ways. The water from one comes from far away, carried through many aqueducts requiring much ingenuity. The source of water for the other one is right beside it and the basin fills soundlessly. The spring is abundant and so the basin spills over and a large stream flows from it. This requires no engineering skills or the construction of conduits. The water just continuously bubbles forth.

I think that the water that comes through the aqueducts is like spiritual consolations in meditation. We draw these consolations through our thoughts. We meditate on created forms to help us, and we fatigue our minds. Finally, through our own efforts, comforting feelings come splashing in, making noise as they fill up the basin.

With the other fountain, the water springs directly from its own source: God. When His Majesty wishes to bless us with supernatural favor, the delight brings with it the greatest peace, quietude, and sweetness to our innermost selves. I don't know where it comes from or how it comes. Earthly consolations are felt in the heart. This kind is not—at least not at first. Later, once the spiritual delight has filled every vessel in the soul, overflowing into all the faculties and each of the dwellings, it reaches the body. That's why I say it starts in God and ends in ourselves. Anyone who has experienced this knows that ultimately our whole outer selves definitely come to enjoy these sweet pleasures.

As I write this, I'm thinking again of that verse I mentioned: *Dilatasti cor meum*, which says that the heart is expanded. But I still don't think this is an experience of the heart. I think its source is much deeper inside. I think it must come from the very core of our being. I have seen secret things in the soul that have left me dumbfounded. And how many more than these must there be!

Oh, my Beloved, my God, how awesome is your grandeur! We walk around down here like silly little shepherds, believing that we are starting to actually know something about you, but it must add up to nothing at all. There are even secrets in our own selves that we cannot fathom. What I mean is that in light of the vastness that is God, our little minds can know "nothing at all." This is not to say that what we do see of you is not extraordinarily wonderful or that your works are anything less than magnificent.

Returning to the biblical passage, what is most useful here, I think, is the part about expansion. As the heavenly water begins to surge from the spring deep inside us, it spreads and expands our whole inner being and gives rise to ineffable blessings. The soul herself cannot even understand what is unfolding here. She senses a certain fragrance, we could say, as if within the depths of her being there were burning coals sprinkled with sweet perfumes. We cannot see the light or locate the source of the fire, but the sweet-smelling warmth permeates the whole of the soul and maybe even spreads into the body.

Look. Try to understand what I'm saying. We don't actually feel heat or smell an aroma. The experience is far more delicate than that. Even if you have not gone through these things yourself, you must know that they really do happen. The soul perceives and understands this more clearly than my mere words could ever express. No matter how intensely we may crave spiritual delight, we cannot acquire it through our own efforts. It is not forged of the same metal that we are but is made from the purest gold of divine wisdom. I don't think the faculties are unified here, but they are absorbed, gazing amazed at what they behold.

It could be that as I write about these matters I am contradicting what I have said in other places. Almost fifteen years have passed since I composed the *Book of My Life* and maybe the Beloved has given me clearer insight about these matters than I had before. Of course, I could be just as mistaken now as I was then. But I could not be lying. By the mercy of God, I would rather die a thousand deaths than lie. I am just sharing what I know to be true.

It seems to me that our will here is in some way united with God's will. But there is no better crucible for testing the genuine value of prayer than the effects and the actions that follow it. If the person receiving this grace recognizes it, then the Beloved is granting her an incredibly great favor. If she doesn't turn back, he is granting her another huge favor.

You will want to attain this depth of prayer yourselves, my friends, and you will be right to want this. The soul can never understand the blessings the Beloved is granting her here or the love with which he is drawing her nearer and nearer to himself. It would be a good thing to know how to obtain this mercy. I'll tell you what I have found out about it.

There are, of course, times when the Beloved grants his blessings for no other reason than simply because he wants to. He knows why, and we shouldn't meddle in this. After you've done what you need to do in the dwellings you've passed through, remember: humility! Humility! This is how the Beloved allows himself to be conquered and will do anything you want. The way you will know if you are humble is that you will not believe that you have earned these mercies and blessings from the Beloved nor that you will ever have them in your whole life.

You will ask me how you will ever attain them if you do not seek them out. My answer is that there is no better way than by not striving. Here are some reasons why.

First, we must love God above all, unmotivated by self-interest.

Second, thinking that in exchange for our insignificant services we are entitled to such a great reward indicates a slight lack of humility.

Third, true preparation for these blessings consists not in the desire for consolations but in the desire to suffer as the Beloved suffered.

Fourth, while His Highness is bound to grant us glory if we keep his commandments, he is not obliged to do us any favors we may crave. Without having our whims satisfied, we can still be liberated. He knows better than we do what is right for us. He knows that we love him. I'm absolutely sure of this. I know people who walk the path of love solely to serve their crucified Christ. Not only do they refuse spiritual delights, but they do not even desire them. In fact, they actually beseech him not to distract them with such pleasures in this lifetime.

The fifth reason we should not strive for spiritual sweetness is that it would be a complete waste of time. This is not the kind of water that is carried through conduits. We accomplish nothing by tiring ourselves out when we cannot draw water from the source. What I mean is that no matter how much we practice meditation, however hard we squeeze ourselves or how many tears we weep, this kind of water doesn't come to us like that. God gives it only to those to whom it is his will to give it, and often when the soul least expects it.

We are his, friends. May he do whatever he pleases with us. May he lead us in ways that best serve him. We must truly humble ourselves and stay detached. I say "truly" because this is not a matter of thinking it. Thought can deceive us. I mean utter humility, complete detachment. Whoever can do this, be assured that the Beloved will not fail to grant her such blessings, and many others she does not even know how to desire.

May he be praised and blessed forever. Amen.

. 3 .

I want to mention a state of prayer that usually comes before the Prayer of Quiet: the Prayer of Recollection.

This is a supernatural recollection. It's not about sitting in the dark or closing your eyes or being subject to any external thing. The eyes close of their own accord and the soul simply desires solitude. It seems that without any intervention a temple is being built through this supernatural recollection where the soul can go to pray. The senses and other external things begin to lose their hold, and the soul starts to recover what she has lost.

It has been said that sometimes the soul enters within herself and sometimes she rises above herself. I wouldn't know how to explain anything with that kind of language.

That's the problem with me: I assume you'll understand things better the way I put them, but maybe I'm only making sense to myself.

Let's say that the senses and the faculties, which are the inhabitants of the interior castle, have gone outside. Let's say they have been hanging around for days and years with strangers who despise all that is beautiful about the castle. When they realize their error, they come back. But before they can reenter the castle, they have to break the bad habits they have been accumulating. They are not traitors. They willingly linger in the vicinity of the castle until they can be allowed in again.

When the great king who is dwelling in the center of the castle perceives their good will, he desires in his wondrous mercy to bring them back to him. He calls to them like a good shepherd beckons his sheep, with a whistle so soft they barely hear it. He teaches them to recognize his voice and discourages them from wandering off and losing their way home to their true abode. The shepherd's call grows so powerful that the ties that had bound the faculties to external things and estranged them from him unravel and they enter the castle.

I don't think I have ever before explained this as clearly as I am describing it now!

As Saint Augustine said after having looked for God in so many places, it is much easier to find God inside ourselves instead of looking for him in created things. It's a big help if God grants us the favor of recollection.

Don't think that the mind can grasp him just by striving

to imagine him dwelling within. This can be an excellent meditation practice, founded on the truth that God is inside us. But it isn't the Prayer of Recollection. Anyone can do this visualization on her own. What I'm talking about is different. These souls may already be inside the castle before they even begin to think about God. I'm not sure how they get in or in what way they hear the shepherd's call. It certainly isn't with the ears, because such a call cannot be perceived through the senses.

How can I make this clearer? Anyone who has gone through it will know what I mean. The soul becomes acutely aware of a gentle withdrawal inside herself. I think I read somewhere a comparison with a hedgehog curling up or a turtle drawing into its shell. But these creatures pull back into themselves whenever they feel like it. Recollection happens only when God wishes to grant us this favor. I myself maintain that His Majesty only gives this gift to those who have already begun to detach from the things of the world. I don't mean that householders should abandon their households, only that they not be obsessed with the mundane. His call to householders is a special one, drawing their attention lovingly inward. I believe that if we long to make a place for the Beloved inside ourselves he will give us this and more, calling our souls higher and higher.

If you have an inner understanding of this, praise God with all your heart. You are right to give thanks for this great favor, and giving thanks opens the door to even greater favors. Certain books teach us that this kind of prayer prepares us for being able to listen to God rather than striving to talk to him. Instead of trying to figure him out, the soul pays attention to whatever it is that the Beloved is working inside her.

Unless His Majesty has begun to absorb us, I don't see how we can put a stop to our minds without actually damaging them. There is a great deal of controversy about this in the spiritual community. I confess my lack of humility here, but no one has succeeded in convincing me of the value of beating the mind into submission. One person tried to use a book written by a man I consider to be a saint, Friar Peter of Alcantara, to talk me into this position. I know that Friar Peter truly understands these matters, and I would have happily conceded except that, as we read the book together, it became evident to us both that he is saying the same thing I am, only with different words. From what he says it is clear that the first thing that needs to happen is for love to be awakened in the soul. I may be mistaken, but here's why I believe in not forcibly trying to curb thought.

The first reason is that, in this work of the spirit, it is the one who thinks less and has the desire to do less that accomplishes more. What we have to do is beg like those who are needy when they come before a wealthy emperor and then lower our gaze and humbly wait. When we realize through his secret ways that he has heard us, then it is best to remain silent. It is enough that he has allowed us to be near him.

Even if we could engage our minds at this time, it would not be wrong to refrain from doing so. But if we are not sure if this king has seen us or heard us, we should not forge ahead foolishly on our own. By struggling to induce this state of prayer, we dry up the soul. By trying not to think, we hopelessly stimulate the imagination. The Beloved wants us to ask him for what we need and be mindful in his presence. He knows what will make us whole. Why should I scramble to make something happen that His Majesty has clearly placed limits on? I'd rather leave the doing to him. There are plenty of other matters he has not reserved for himself, like renunciation, acts of charity, and devotional prayer. We can do these things on our own, to the extent that our nature permits, and always, of course, with the help of his loving hand.

The second reason is that all these inner activities are gentle and serene. To do anything painful would cause more harm than good. What I mean by painful is anything that we try to coerce ourselves into doing. Think about how much it starts to hurt to hold your breath, for instance. Leave your soul in God's hands. Let him do whatever he wants with her. Detach as radically as you are able from your own benefit and surrender to the will of God.

The third reason is that the harder you try not to think of anything, the more aroused your mind will become and you will think even more.

The fourth is that what is most essential and pleasing to God is that we remember him and forget ourselves, and that we honor him and relinquish our own pleasure and comfort. But how can we forget ourselves when we are being obsessively careful not to stir our minds or desires? Such stirring can actually awaken powerful longing for God and serve as the catalyst for spontaneously praising the glory that is his. When His Majesty is ready for the mind to grow still, he engages it in another way and illumines the consciousness so completely that it remains absorbed. Then, without knowing how it happened, the mind is taught much more skillfully than we could have ever taught it on our own by trying to make it not think! Didn't God give us our faculties to work with and isn't this work our reward? There is no point in trying to trick them. Let them do their appointed task until God assigns them a higher one.

What I understand is that the best thing to do is to endeavor, without any strain or clamoring, to stem the flow of thoughts but not to shut down the mind or suspend consciousness. It's important to be aware that you are in God's presence and remember who this God is. If this remembrance alters the consciousness, so be it. But the soul shouldn't try to analyze the state she's in; it is a gift given to the will, not the intellect. Let the soul enjoy it without any effort beyond a few loving words. Even if you are not actively trying to keep yourself from thinking in this state, thoughts often cease by themselves here, at least for a moment.

Remember: this kind of prayer flows as a natural spring, rather than being channeled through manufactured conduits. The mind is restrained, here. Maybe it restrains itself. It realizes that it doesn't know what it wants. It wanders from one extreme to another, like a fool who cannot find his assigned seat.

What I am talking about now is the kind of prayer I started off with in my discussion of this dwelling. I should have described the Prayer of Recollection first, which is far less profound than the prayer of spiritual sweetness I spoke of before, which I have sometimes referred to as the Prayer of Quiet. But it is the first step to this higher state. In the Prayer of Recollection it isn't necessary to abandon discursive meditation or mental activity.

Ultimately, the will rests so deeply in God that the pandemonium inside the mind is very bothersome to the soul. But if she pays too much attention to this disturbance she will lose the sweetness she is enjoying. She must forget about all the turmoil and let herself down into the arms of God. His Majesty will teach the soul what to do next. It's all about recognizing her own limitations in the face of such great goodness and occupying herself with giving thanks.

In dealing with the Prayer of Recollection, I neglected to mention the signs by which we may know that God, our Beloved, is blessing the soul with the Prayer of Quiet. Clearly, an expansion of the soul takes place, as if the water rising up from the fountain doesn't just overflow and move on. Instead, the more water that comes up, the larger the basin grows to receive it. That's what this kind of prayer does to the soul. And God works many other wonders in her, shaping and preparing her to contain abundant grace.

This sweet inner expansion frees the soul from constraints in her service to God. She is no longer oppressed by fear of the underworld. Although she desires more than ever not to offend God, she is anything but groveling now. She is fully confident that she will find her delight in him. While she used to be afraid of austerities, concerned that they would compromise her delicate health, now she knows that in God she can do everything. Her desire for self-sacrifice is much greater than before. She no longer worries about trials. Her faith is revitalized. She understands that any hardships she suffers are for God and that His Majesty will give her the grace to bear them patiently. Sometimes she will even desire tribulation because of this intense longing to do something for God.

As her awareness of the greatness of God increases, the soul more clearly perceives her own imperfections. Since she has tasted spiritual sweetness, worldly pleasures look like garbage. She finds herself withdrawing from them little by little and gradually gaining some mastery over herself. All her virtues increase and will continue to grow even stronger as long as she doesn't turn back and offend God. If she does, she will lose everything, no matter how high up the mountain she has climbed. Please don't assume that just because God has granted the soul this favor once or twice all these wonderful things will automatically unfold. The soul has to be actively open to them and maintain her openness. All our good lies in perseverance.

If you find yourself in this state, I strongly offer you this advice: be exceedingly conscious of the devotion you owe God and avoid any opportunity to jeopardize your commitment to him. At this point, the soul is a baby not yet ready to be weaned. If she turns away from her mother's breasts, what can she be expected to do but die? This is what I'm afraid will happen to you on a spiritual level if you have been granted the mercy of this nurturing prayer and then give up on it. If you don't have some excellent reason for withdrawing from prayer and if you don't come back quickly, you will go from bad to worse. I know that you will share my deep fear of this.

I have watched certain people turn away from the One who, with pure love, yearned to be their friend and prove his friendship with divine action. I feel so sorry for people like this! Those of you who have been graced by this state of prayer are even more vulnerable than the majority of souls who have not been granted such a favor by the Beloved. Be extra careful to avoid occasions for error. The spirit of evil will try much harder to capture one soul so touched by God than ten thousand souls who have not been. Such a soul can do a great deal of damage to the spirit of evil by attracting others through her example away from unconsciousness and into the light of the spiritual life. The spirit of evil may have no other reason to take interest in such a soul than the fact that His Highness has shown her special love. But that's enough for the spirit of evil to burn himself out trying to lead her to perdition!

You, friends, seem to be free of dangers like these. May God keep you safe from pride and vanity. You will know if the spirit of evil is trying to offer you counterfeit versions of God's favors by their effects: they will be the opposite to the effects of divine blessings.

There is a danger I have seen women in particular suc-
cumb to that I need to warn you about. Because of our inherent tenderness, we are more likely to face this situation. That
is, some women weaken their health by overdoing prayer,
fasting, and severe austerities. Then, when they do receive
some divine favor, they are overwhelmed. An inner sense of
consolation is reflected in an outer weakness and swooning.
They collapse into a state of unconsciousness they consider
to be a spiritual trance and let themselves drown in it. The
more they give in to this, the more dissociated they become
and their constitution gets even weaker.

These people think that they are being carried away by
rapture; I call it carried away by foolishness. All they are
doing is wasting time and wrecking their health. Their senses
are not transcended and they are feeling nothing of God,
either.

One person remained in this state for eight hours. Fortunately, there was someone who understood her. By getting
her to quit doing penance and start to eat and sleep, she
snapped her out of her stupor. Without meaning any harm,
this person had misled her spiritual guides and deceived herself. I believe that the spirit of evil would do anything to get
to such souls, and he was making significant inroads with
this one.

Please understand that when something truly comes
from God there may be an inner and outer languor, but there
will be no languishing in the soul. When she finds herself

close to God, the soul is deeply moved. This experience does not linger but passes all too quickly. Although she is likely to become absorbed again, the absorption is not caused by weakness. It does not wear down the body or create any particular external sensations.

Take my advice: if you start to feel this swooning, tell your spiritual guide and then try to do something for fun. Your guide should urge you to radically reduce the number of hours you spend in spiritual practice and try to make you eat well and get some sleep until your natural health returns.

If this doesn't work, it might be the case that you just don't have the constitution for a contemplative path. Maybe God wants you to worship him through an active life. People like this are needed in spiritual communities. Keep yourself busy with different duties and try to avoid too much solitude or you will ruin your health. You might feel ashamed of this lifestyle, but the Beloved is testing your love for him by seeing how you bear his absence. After a while, he will give you back the strength to feel him close again. Even if he doesn't, what you gain through surrender and prescribed rituals will benefit you as much as or more than what you would have earned in other ways.

I know some people who have such weak minds and poor imaginations that they believe that everything that pops into their heads manifests. That kind of delusion can be very dangerous, as I will explain later. Since this is the dwelling that most souls enter, I have gone into greater detail about it.

This is the place where the natural and the supernatural commingle, and so the spirit of evil can get in and do some real harm. In the dwellings to come, the Beloved doesn't allow him such easy access.

May God be forever praised. Amen.

Fifth Dwelling

❧

. I .

Oh, friends! How could I ever describe the riches, the treasures and delights to be found inside the fifth dwelling? There is no way of knowing how to talk about such things, and so I almost think it would be better to remain silent. The mind cannot grasp them. Metaphors are useless since no earthly image is subtle or sublime enough for this purpose.

Send light from heaven, my Beloved, so that I might be able to enlighten your servants. Some of them have often tasted these delights. Don't let them be deceived when the spirit of evil masquerades as an angel of light. All they care about is pleasing you.

Even though I only referred to "some of your servants,"

the truth is that there are not very many who fail to gain entrance to these dwellings. They attain to different levels, but most of them make their way in somehow or another. Very few will experience the things I am about to describe, but if they even reach the threshold, God is granting them bountiful mercy. Although many are called, few are chosen.

All of us who wear the sacred robes of this sisterhood are answering the call to prayer and contemplative practice. We trace our lineage to those holy fathers and mothers from Mount Carmel who rejected the world, embraced solitude, and went seeking this precious pearl of contemplation. Yet so few of us are actually open to receiving it from the Beloved's hands. Externally, we are doing all the right things. But we need to do much, much more on an inner level to reach the heights of righteousness. We cannot afford to be careless in any way.

So let's stop for a minute now, friends, be courageous, and demand that the Beloved give us his grace so that if anything is missing it is not our fault. To the extent that we can experience heaven here on earth, let him strengthen our souls and show us the way so that we can excavate this hidden treasure. The truth is, the treasure is inside of us.

I said "strengthen our souls" to remind you that if God does not give you physical strength, it doesn't matter. Anyone can purchase this treasure from him. All you have to do is offer everything you have and God is content. Blessed be so great a God! But reflect on this, friends: if you wish to enjoy his blessings, hold nothing back. Whether you have a little or a lot, he wants it all. In proportion to what you have given, he will grant you greater or lesser favors. This is the test for proving whether we have attained the Prayer of Union.

Don't think that this union is some kind of dreamy state like the one I was talking about earlier. The reason I would even use the term "dream" is that the soul seems to fall asleep. But she is neither sleeping nor awake. It's the faculties that are asleep in this state—deeply asleep—to things of the world and to the self. In fact, during the short time the Prayer of Union lasts, the soul transcends both sense and reason. She couldn't think a single thought even if she wanted to. Any prescribed technique for suspending consciousness is rendered utterly unnecessary.

Even if she is able to love, she does not understand in the midst of her loving how or what it is she loves. She doesn't know what she wants. She has died completely to this world so that she can fully live in God. This is a delicious death. It is as if the soul were being plucked out of all of the activities of life on earth. And it is a delightful death. The soul is so withdrawn from the body that I don't know how she is left with enough life even to breathe. I was pondering this just now and have come to the conclusion that she isn't. At least, if she is still breathing, she is entirely unaware of it.

The mind desperately wants to be involved in understanding something of what the soul is feeling. But it is not strong enough for this, and so it remains stunned. Even if the soul does not totally lose consciousness, she can't move a hand or a foot. She resembles a person who has fallen into such a deep faint that it seems like he's dead.

Oh, the secrets of God! If I thought I could succeed in conveying them to you I would never get tired of trying. And so I will say a thousand things wrong in hopes that I might get something right and we can praise the Lord with all our hearts.

I say that the Prayer of Union is not some kind of dream state because the soul maintains a certain level of skepticism about the experience she is having in this dwelling. Is she imagining this union? Maybe she fell asleep. Or perhaps the experience really is a gift from God. On the other hand, the spirit of evil might have transformed itself into an angel of light to trick her. The soul suffers from a thousand suspicions. And it is a good thing to be suspicious here. Even our own natures can sometimes fool us in this dwelling.

Although there is not much room here for poisonous creatures to enter, a few tiny lizards do get in here. These reptiles have such slender heads they can poke them in anywhere. If we pay no attention to them, they can do no harm. These are the small thoughts that breed in the imagination; they are more of an annoyance than anything else.

Eventually, deep into the fifth dwelling, even these agile reptiles can't slip in. Neither imagination nor memory nor the discursive intellect can impede the blessing. I would go so far as to say that if this Prayer of Union is truly union with God, even the spirit of evil cannot find its way in to hurt us. His Majesty is so entwined and unified with the essence of the soul that the spirit of evil would not dare come near and would never understand the secrets unfolding there even if it did. It's obvious. If the spirit of evil can't know our thoughts, how could it ever begin to grasp something so secret that God doesn't even entrust this understanding to our own minds?

Oh, what great goodness comes from this state in which the unholy energies can do us no harm! The soul is utterly blessed to have God work with her in such a way that no one can disturb him—not even the soul herself. What will he, who so loves giving and can give all he wants, not give?

I wonder if I have confused you by saying "if this prayer is truly union with God," implying that there are other varieties of union. Well, there are! If we are overly attached to vapid vanities, the spirit of evil will use them to transport us. But it does not do it the way God does it. It doesn't fill the soul with that same sweet delight and satisfaction. It doesn't transport her with that pure peace and joy. True union transcends all earthly joys, exceeds all earthly delights, surpasses all earthly satisfactions. And it is beyond even all that. You can tell from experience that this joy has a very different source of origin. I once said that the difference is like feeling something with the skin of your body or down in the marrow of your bones. I think that hits the nail on the head; I don't think I could say it any better than that.

Are you still unsatisfied? Are you afraid that these inner realities are so difficult to examine that you can all too easily be mistaken? For anyone who has experienced this blessing, what I have said will ring true. But let me offer a clear sign so that you won't be left with any room for doubt about whether or not this is a favor that comes from God. His Majesty has just reminded me of this today, and I think it settles the whole issue.

Even if I believe that I understand what I'm talking about and that I'm telling the truth, I always preface it with "I think" or "it seems to me." I know that I may be mistaken, and so I am quite prepared to listen to those who have studied these matters deeply. Even if they have not experienced these states themselves, very learned men have a certain sensibility that guides them. Since God has given them the job of shedding light on spiritual subjects, he enlightens them so that they will recognize truth when they encounter it. But if they are truly God's servants and do not dissipate their gifts, they will never be surprised by any manifestation of his greatness. They will know well that he is capable of this and ever so much more. Besides, even if some things are not readily explained, learned men can find other references in their books to indicate that these sorts of things do happen.

I have had a great deal of experience with men of learning. I have also had experience with half-learned men who are full of fear and have cost me dearly. It is my opinion that anyone who does not believe that God can do this and so much more, and that he is pleased to sometimes grant such blessings to his creatures, has closed the door on receiving these blessings himself.

Don't let this happen to you, friends. Believe in God more and more deeply. Don't presume to make judgments about the ones he transmits his favors to as being good souls or bad. I have told you: only His Majesty knows this. Our intervention is unnecessary. All we need to do is to serve him and praise him for his works and wonders, with humility and simplicity of heart.

Let's return to that sign I mentioned which cannot fail to convince us that the union is real. God has made the soul into an utter fool so that he can replace false intelligence with true wisdom. In a state of union, the soul sees nothing and hears nothing and comprehends nothing. Union lasts such a short time, and it seems even shorter than it really is. God presses himself so fully against the inside of the soul that when she returns to herself the soul has no doubt whatsoever that God was in her and she was in God. This truth remains with her forever. Even though years may go by without God granting this blessing again, the soul can never forget. She never doubts: God was in her; she was in God. This knowingness is all that matters.

How, you might ask, could the soul see this truth and understand it if she is incapable of seeing or understanding anything? Well, it is not in the moment of union that the soul is cognizant of this truth, but she sees it clearly afterwards. It isn't some vision that convinces her. It is an unshakable certainty, and God himself has put it there.

I know a person who hadn't learned that God's presence and power and essence is in all things. Then, God granted her this favor, and she knew it with perfect certitude. She asked one of these half-learned men about how God is in us and we are in God. But he knew as little as she had before her enlightenment. He told her that, only through grace, God comes to us on rare occasions and is not an abiding companion. She didn't believe him. The truth had been firmly planted in her soul. She asked some others who confirmed her truth and this was deeply consoling to her.

Don't be mistaken. This conviction is not built upon any physical forms. It is not like the invisible presence of our Beloved Jesus Christ in the most holy sacrament. It has nothing to do with manifestation; it's purely about divinity. How is it, then, that we are so fully convinced of what we cannot see? I don't know. These are the works of God. What I do know is that I am telling the truth. Whoever does not possess this certainty has not, I believe, experienced union of the whole soul with God. Maybe she experienced union of one of the faculties. Or maybe God granted her a few of the many other blessings he gives to souls. We need to stop looking for reasons to explain how all these blessings happen. Our minds cannot grasp these things, anyway. Isn't it enough to know that he who causes all this is omnipotent? It is God who does it. No matter how much energy we expend, we have nothing to do with making this happen. We need to give up our desire to comprehend divine blessings.

I just remembered when the bride says in the Song of Songs: the king brought me into the wine cellar (or put me in it, I think it says). It doesn't say that she *went*. It also says that she wandered around looking for her Beloved everywhere. I see union as the wine cellar where the Beloved puts us when he wishes and how he wishes. But no matter how hard we try, we can't get in on our own. His Majesty must place us right in the center of our own soul and then enter us himself. Our will surrenders to him without reservation. Without the active functioning of our will, he can clearly reveal his wonders. The faculties and the senses, too, are asleep, and he doesn't want the door to them opened. He enters the center of the soul without any door, like Christ did when he came to his disciples and said, *Pax vobis,* and when he left the tomb without rolling away the boulder.

Oh, friends! There is so much that we will see as long as we do not desire to see more than our own limitations allow and we accept that we may not be ready to receive such a great Beloved and if we acknowledge that we are incapable of comprehending his wonders.

May he be forever praised. Amen.

You may think that everything there is to say about the fifth dwelling has already been said. Far from it. I told you: people experience different levels of this place. I don't think I can say much more about the nature of union. But there are many things I could say about the wonders the Beloved begins to work inside the soul once she has prepared herself for his blessing. To help you visualize the state of the soul here, I offer a metaphor. It may help you see that while there's not a thing we can do to direct the work of the Beloved, there is much we can do to open ourselves to receiving his favors.

You must have heard about the incredible way that silk comes into being. What a marvelous example of his wonders in creation! Only God could have invented something like this. It all begins with little grains, something like pepper-corns. I have never seen this, by the way, but only heard about it, so if I get some of the details wrong it isn't my fault. Any-way, as the weather gets warmer and the mulberry tree starts to leaf out, the seeds are quickened with new life. It had seemed that these nuggets were dead, but now they stir and begin to nourish themselves on the sustenance of the mul-berry leaves. Soon they grow to full size. That's when they settle down onto some twigs and begin to spin silk with their tiny mouths. They weave these little silken cocoons and trap themselves inside them. After a while, the plump and homely worm emerges as a graceful white butterfly.

Now if this had never been witnessed by anyone but had been passed down by oral tradition from ancient times, who would believe it? Who could possibly convince us that a crea-ture as devoid of reason as a bug could be so diligent and industrious in working for our benefit? And, in the end, the poor little worm loses its life for its efforts. Even if I were not to say another word, friends, this thought alone is worthy of a meditation session. In this image you can see reflected the wonders and wisdom of our God. Can you imagine if we were able to know the true attributes of everything? It's very beneficial for us to intentionally ponder these wonderful things. We can't help but rejoice in being the brides of a king so powerful and wise.

The silkworm is like the soul. She comes alive with the heat of the Holy Spirit and begins to accept the help God is offering. She starts to make use of the remedies available in spiritual community, things like ritual, sacred literature, inspiring talks. These are medicines that can cure a soul that has been deadened by carelessness and unconsciousness, a soul struggling against the constant opportunity for error. Sustained by the food of good meditations, the soul grows and thrives. This growth is what matters here; everything else is irrelevant.

And so when the silkworm is fully developed it begins to build the house where it will die. I would like to point out that this house is Christ. It seems to me that I read or heard somewhere that our life is hidden in God or that our life *is* God. The exact source of this quote is unimportant. Think of our silkworm.

Don't you see then, my friends, what we can do with the help of God? In the Prayer of Union, His Majesty himself becomes the dwelling we spin for ourselves. Since I am saying that he is the dwelling we build to place ourselves inside, it may sound like I'm suggesting that we can build God up and then take him away again. Well, we can! It's not that we can add to or subtract from God, but we can take away from ourselves and build up a house for him, just like these little silkworms do. Before we can even finish doing all that we can do, God will take this insignificant contribution of ours and unite it with his greatness, rendering it of such excellent value that the Beloved offers himself as our reward. He's the one who paid the highest price in the first place. Now the Beloved wants to join our small labors with the enormous trials he suffered so that his efforts and ours become one.

So let's get on with it, my friends! Let's do the work quickly and spin the silken cocoon, relinquishing our self-centeredness and personal willfulness and giving up our attachment to worldly things. Let's practice humility, prayer, purification, surrender, and all the other good works we're familiar with. We have learned exactly what to do. Let's do it! Let it die. Let the silkworm die. This is the natural outcome once it has done what it was created to do. Then we will see God and see ourselves nestled inside his greatness like the silkworm in her cocoon. Remember that when I say we "see God," I mean in the sense in which he allows himself to be seen in this kind of union.

Everything I've been saying leads up to what becomes of the silkworm. The soul in this state of prayer dies to the world and emerges a little white butterfly. Oh, the greatness of God! How magnificent that the soul, having been hidden in the greatness of God and so closely joined with him, is so transformed. This union, I believe, is very short. I don't think it ever lasts longer than a half an hour. I'm telling you: the soul doesn't recognize herself anymore. Think of the difference between an unsightly worm and a white butterfly. That's how different the soul is after her transformation of union.

The soul cannot imagine how she could deserve such a blessing. She finds herself overflowing with a desire to praise the Lord. She longs for annihilation. She would gladly die a thousand deaths for him. She is completely willing to suffer any trials presented to her. Her desire for renunciation and solitude grows deeper. All she wishes is that every sentient being could know God. It torments her to see her Beloved dishonored in any way.

See the restlessness of this little butterfly now and praise God for it! Although she is calmer and quieter than she has ever been in her life, she doesn't know where to settle down and make her home. After the refuge she has known, everything on earth is dissatisfying, especially if God has served her his sweet wine again and again, bringing with it new blessings almost every time. She does not think much anymore of the work she did as a worm. Who cares about weaving a cocoon strand by strand when you have wings? How could she be happy creeping step by step when she can fly? Compared to the intensity of her longing to serve God, anything she can do for him looks meager in her own eyes. She's not even that impressed by what the saints endured, now that she understands through experience how the Beloved helps and transforms a soul. She no longer recognizes the reflection of her own image.

Remember the weakness the soul used to suffer when she practiced austerities? Now this becomes her strength. Remember her attachment to friends and relatives or to wealth and possessions? It used to be that no matter what she did or how strong her determination was or how deeply she desired to withdraw from the world, it never seemed to be enough to loosen her grip; in fact it felt to her that she grew more attached to everything. Now it pains her to have to fulfill her obligations in those arenas, but she knows she must tend them because she is committed to honoring God in all things. It all makes her weary. She has discovered that she can never find true rest in created things.

Although it may seem to you like I am getting a little carried away by this subject, anyone who has received this favor from God will see that I have barely touched it. It is no surprise that this little butterfly who feels so estranged from the world begins to seek true refuge again. But where can the poor creature go? She can't return to where she came from. No matter how hard we try, we are powerless to enter God's abode until he is pleased to bring us there again himself.

Oh, Beloved! What new trials begin to unfold for this soul? Who could imagine that such suffering could be possible after so sublime an encounter? But as long as we live, there will be crosses to bear. If anyone reported to me that after arriving here she sustained a state of rest and bliss from then on, I would say that she had not actually reached this place. Maybe she got as far as the dwelling before this one and experienced some kind of spiritual consolation there which was enhanced by her natural weakness. Maybe it was even the spirit of evil feeding false peace to the soul so that it could shatter her later with an even more savage attack.

I don't mean to say that those who arrive here have no peace. They do have peace, deep peace. Because the trials they go through, although severe, are so valuable and their source so excellent, they do bring tranquility and contentment to the soul. Yet out of her unhappiness with worldly things arises an intensely painful longing to leave this world.

The thought that it must be God's will for the soul to be living this life of exile comforts her a little, but not enough. In spite of all she's been through, the soul is not yet completely surrendered to God's will, though she strives to align herself with it. But she accompanies this effort with many tears. She is stricken with remorse that she can do no more because she has not been given the ability to do more. She holds the pain of this in her heart every time she is in prayer.

Maybe this sorrow arises from looking upon a world that does not love God enough. So many people seem lost in unconsciousness! This soul knows that God's mercy is infinite and no matter how caught in illusion these people may be they can always wake up and be liberated, but she is still afraid that many of them will be lost forever.

Oh, greatness of God! Only a few years ago—maybe even days—the soul wasn't aware of anything but herself. Who is it that has plunged her into such excruciating anxiety? Even if we tried meditating day and night, we wouldn't feel this as acutely as this soul is feeling it now. God help me! If I were to reflect for many days and years on the error of not loving God, would that be enough? If I were to reflect for many days and years on the fact that those who fail to love him are his children, and my own brothers and sisters, would that be enough? If I were to reflect for many days and years on the perils we live with and on how good it will be to leave this relative world behind, would it be enough? No, it would not, friends. The grief here is nothing like the grief there. With the Beloved's help, we can touch the surface of that grief through profound meditation, but it doesn't reach the depths of our being as it does in that exalted state. Here it breaks the soul and grinds her to dust without the soul ever striving for anything or even wanting it at all. Where does such pain come from? I'll tell you.

Remember when I said that God brought the bride into the innermost wine cellar? What I didn't mention is that this is where he invested her with charity. Now the soul's great love for God moves her to surrender herself so completely into his hands that, in the deep peace that comes with this surrender, she neither knows nor desires anything beyond that his will be done.

I don't believe that God would ever grant this favor except to a soul that he has taken for his very own. It is God's will that, without the soul understanding how it has happened, she go forth from union with his seal impressed upon her. That's all the soul does in this union, anyway: no more than the wax does when it receives the impression of a seal. The wax doesn't press the seal into itself! It stays soft; it yields. And even in yielding it doesn't soften itself. It just remains still and gives its consent.

Oh, the goodness of God! Everything must come to us at such a high cost to you! All you want is what we want. All you want is that there be no obstruction in the wax.

And so you see, friends, what God does here so that the soul will recognize herself as his. He gives her something of his own, just as he gave to his Son when he walked this world. He cannot grant us a higher favor than that. Who could have wanted to leave this life more fervently than his Son did? That's what he meant at the Last Supper when he said, "With desire have I desired."

I ask you, my Love, did it occur to you that you were about to face an excruciating and laborious death? Did it terrify you? No, you answer, because my great love and the desire I have for souls to be liberated utterly transcend that pain. The most intense desire I have suffered since I lived in the world melts to nothing in the warmth of this love.

I have often pondered this truth. There is a certain soul I know who suffers terribly whenever she sees that the Beloved is being dishonored. Her pain is so intense that she'd rather die than endure it. Compared to the charity of Christ, this soul's charity is minuscule. And so if she experiences this torment as unbearable, what must our Beloved Jesus Christ have felt? What kind of existence must he have suffered, since absolutely everything was clear to him and he was continuously witnessing terrible offenses being committed against his Father?

I believe that this anguish was much greater than his Passion. In the midst of his Passion, he could already see an end to his trials. This glimmer of imminent emancipation, along with the joy he felt at knowing that his death would serve as a remedy for the rest of us, plus knowing that he was a living example of perfect love for his Father through suffering perfectly for him, combined to temper his agony.

And so it is here. When those who have grown strong in love practice renunciation, they rarely feel pain. In fact, their sacrifices seem petty to them and they wish to do more and more. What must the Beloved have felt to have been given this peerless opportunity to demonstrate his perfect obedience to his Father and his unconditional love for his neighbor?

What sweet delight to suffer in doing the will of God! Still, to continuously see His Majesty dishonored and to watch so many souls fall into unconsciousness must have been so horrific that, if he had been no more than human, I believe that one day of that pain would have been a hot enough fire to obliterate not just a single but multiple lifetimes.

.3.

Now let's see what has become of our little butterfly. She is striving to move ever forward in self-knowledge and in service to her Beloved. God has been very good to her. Still, she can't just passively receive divine favor and presume complete security. She must not grow careless and wander off the heavenly path. It takes conscious intention to keep the commandments. Otherwise, what happens to the silkworm will happen to the soul.

Once the silkworm has sown the seeds that will sprout new silkworms, it dies forever. I say that it "sows seeds" because it is my strong belief that God does not grant such favors in vain. If a person does not benefit directly from it, then the favor will benefit somebody else. God's blessing leaves exalted desires inside the soul, which cause her to live righteously and give generously to others. From contact with her fire, other souls will ignite. And even when the flames in the soul have cooled, her inclination to help others remains and she delights in describing the favors God gives to whoever loves him and serves him.

I know a certain person who went through this. She had drifted astray, but she was still happy to help others with the gifts God had given her. She taught the way of prayer to those who did not understand it, and it did them a great deal of good. Later, the Beloved gave her light again. It's true that this person had not experienced the full spectrum of effects we have been talking about. But think of all those souls called by God to be witnesses like Judas was, or to be kings like Saul was, and then through their own unconsciousness fell off the path.

And so what this reminds us, friends, is that if we don't want to get lost like them and we do want to grow in virtue, our safety lies in steadfast surrender to the will of God. I'm talking to those of you to whom he has granted such favors. Actually, I'm talking to everyone!

It seems to me that in spite of all I've said about this mansion, something of it remains obscure. It's obvious that great good comes to souls who make it to this place of prayer, but I don't want to give you the impression that you are hopeless if God has not granted you these supernatural gifts. True union is always available, with God's help. What we need to do is to set our intention to attain it by tying our will unconditionally to the will of God. Oh, how many of us there are who claim to do this! We believe that there is nothing else we want and that we would die for this truth. Well, I will tell you now and tell you again later: if you have received this blessing from the Beloved and your will is irrevocably resigned to God's will, then you won't even care about that sweet union we've been discussing. The most important thing about that union is that it arises from melding with the divine will, anyway.

Oh, how precious is that union! How blessed is the soul who has reached it! She will dwell in serenity in this life and in the next. Nothing in the world will cause her to lose her equanimity, unless she finds herself at risk of breaking her connection with God or sees that her Beloved is being dishonored in some way. She deals peacefully with poverty, sickness, and even death—except for the death of a true spiritual companion. The soul sees clearly that God knows what he is doing better than she knows what she is wanting.

You should realize that there are different kinds of grief. Sometimes we are struck suddenly and grief rises naturally out of our humanity, just as pleasure does. Sometimes charity and compassion for other sentient beings stirs grief in our hearts. This is what moved Christ to raise Lazarus from the dead. Union with the will of God does not preclude such feelings. But this grief does not disquiet the soul with restless passion; it passes swiftly. Remember how I said that spiritual consolations in prayer only seem to reach the faculties and do not touch the still depths of the soul? So it is with this kind of suffering.

Bear in mind, friends: the silkworm must die. This death is at your expense. But union with the Beloved reveals that a new life is about to unfold, and this glimpse helps tremendously with your dying. For now it is our job to live this life fully and put the silkworm to death consciously. I confess that killing the silkworm requires inordinate effort, but it's worth it; if you succeed, your reward will be manifold.

You have no reason to doubt the possibility of true union with the will of God. This is the union I have longed for all my life. This is the union for which I pray without ceasing. This is the union that is clear and secure.

But, sadly for us, very few ever attain it. We delude ourselves into believing that if we simply embark on a spiritual journey and honor God with care, we have done all that we need to do. But there are always a few little insects lurking unrecognized until they have gnawed through our virtues. The damage happens through subtle self-centeredness, judging others in insidious little ways, neglecting to cultivate compassion, and forgetting to love our neighbor as ourselves. Even though we may plod along doing what we think is expected of us and not technically committing any sins, we don't make much progress toward uniting ourselves with the will of God.

What do you think his will is, friends? I think that it is that we attain perfect union with him. I tell you, it hurts me intensely to write this, because I see how far from this perfection I am myself, and the fault is all my own. God is under no obligation to bestow great gifts to motivate us. Isn't it enough that he has offered us his Son to show us the way? Do not think that this is a matter of being so aligned with the will of God that if my father or my daughter die I don't grieve, or that if trials or illnesses come up I suffer them cheerfully. A positive attitude is a good thing, and sometimes we have no choice and so we make a virtue out of necessity. The philosophers did this by making the most of their wisdom.

On the spiritual path, the Beloved asks only two things of us: that we love him and that we love each other. This is all we have to strive for. If we do these perfectly, we are doing his will and so we will be united with him. But we are far from being able to do the things we ought to do for such a great God. May it please His Majesty to give us the grace to desire to do whatever is necessary to reach a state that is, in fact, in our power to reach!

In my opinion, the most reliable sign that we are following both of these teachings is that we are loving each other. Although we might have some clear indications that we are loving God, we can't be sure that we really are, but it is obvious whether or not we are loving each other. Be assured that the more progress you make in loving your neighbor, the greater will be your love for God. His Majesty loves us so much that he repays us for loving our neighbor by increasing our love for him in a thousand ways. I cannot doubt this.

It is important that we walk this path of love mindfully. If we practice love to perfection, we will have done all that there is to do. Because human nature is flawed, I don't believe that we could ever achieve perfect love for our neighbor unless the love that blossoms is rooted in God.

Since this path is so important, friends, let's try to understand ourselves better—even in the smallest ways—and be discriminating about all the big plans that sometimes swarm in our minds during prayer when we think of all the wonders we will do for love of our neighbors or even for that one identified soul we are going to charge forth and save. If our actions later are not in harmony with these ideas, why believe that we could ever bring them to fruition?

The same thing is true for humility and all the other virtues. The spirit of evil is crafty. If it thinks that it can trick us into believing that we have a single virtue that we do not in fact have, it will run around hell a thousand times to do so. And it would be correct in assuming that this delusion would do us harm. Imaginary virtues are always accompanied by a certain arrogance. The virtues God gives us are unencumbered by pride.

It amuses me sometimes to see certain souls who, when they are in prayer, profess that they would gladly be humiliated and suffer public shame for the sake of God and then afterwards try to hide the tiniest fault. Or if they are accused of doing something bad which they haven't done, God save us! Anyone who cannot bear trials like these should be especially careful to ignore the grand resolutions she conjures up for herself in prayer. Her determination does not rise authentically from the will but rather is an artifact of the imagination.

This is the most fertile place for the spirit of evil to cultivate its tricks and deceptions. For those of us who aren't sure of the respective functions of our different faculties, or are ignorant of many other interior matters, this can be a serious problem.

Oh, friends! I can clearly see how important love of your neighbor is to some of you, and how others of you just don't seem to care. If only you could understand how vital this virtue is to all of us, you wouldn't engage in any other study.

Sometimes I observe people so diligently trying to orchestrate whatever state of prayer they're in that they become peevish about it. They don't dare to move or let their minds be stirred for fear of jeopardizing the slightest degree of devotion or delight. It makes me realize how little they understand of the path to union. They think the whole thing is about rapture.

But no, friends, no! What the Beloved wants from us is action. What he wants is that if one of your friends is sick, you take care of her. Don't worry about interrupting your devotional practice. Have compassion. If she is in pain, you feel it, too. If necessary, you fast so she can eat. This is not a matter of indulging an individual; you do it because you know it is your Beloved's desire. This is true union with his will. What he wants is for you to be much happier hearing some-one else praised than you would be to receive a compliment yourself. If you have humility, this is easy. It is a great thing to be glad when your friends' virtues are celebrated, and when you see a fault in another it is good to be as sorry as if it were your own and to make an effort to conceal it.

May it please the Beloved that we never fail to love each other, because if we do we are lost. If we succeed in loving each other, I tell you we will attain union with him. Never cease striving for this. Maybe you have had some gratifying experiences that have awakened some devotion in your heart so that you believe you have reached this state. Maybe in the Prayer of Quiet you achieved moments of sweet suspension. People often assume that this means they have reached their goal. But believe me, if you are not loving your neighbor you have not attained union.

Beseech our Beloved to give you the capacity for perfect love. Allow His Majesty to work freely in you. If you strive to do whatever you can about this love, he will give you more than you can even desire. Urge yourself to respond to the needs of your friends even if this means forfeiting your own rights. No matter how much your nature may resist, forget your own good for their sake. When the occasion arises, try to take up some burden to relieve your neighbor of it. Don't think that this is a path of convenience or that you will find everything done for you. Look at the price our Beloved Spouse paid for his love. He died an agonizing death on the cross so that we could be free from dying.

.4.

You must be getting curious about what this little butter-fly is doing now, since I told you that it is impossible for her to find rest in worldly pleasures or in spiritual consola-tions. She flies higher than all that. I cannot satisfy your curiosity about this until we get to the final dwelling. May God grant that I remember it then and have time to write about it! Five months have passed since I began this assignment and because my head is in no shape to read it all over again I will undoubtedly continue in a disorderly fashion and probably say some of the same things twice. Because this is written for my friends, this shouldn't be too much of a problem.

I still want to say more to you about what the Prayer of Union is. Since it is my style to use metaphors, I will continue to talk about the little butterfly. She is always fruitful in the good she does for other souls and for herself. But she cannot find a place to let down and rest.

You've often heard it said that God spiritually betroths himself to souls. Blessed be his mercy that he is pleased to be so humble. The comparison is a crude one, but the sacrament of marriage is as close as I can come to evoking the bonding that unfolds between the soul and God. The difference is that human marriage contains all things while in this spiritual wedding nothing remains that is anything other than spiritual. Pleasures of the body have little to do with this union; the spiritual delights the Beloved shares with the soul are a thousand leagues removed from the pleasures married people must experience. It is all about love melting into love. Its expression is absolutely pure, exceedingly delicate, and gentle. There is no way to describe it, but the Beloved knows how to make it deeply felt.

It seems to me that the Prayer of Union does not quite reach the point of spiritual betrothal. It's more like what occurs here on earth when two people are in the process of considering marriage. There is a discussion about how compatible they are, if they are in love, and how they can spend time getting to know each other better so that they can appreciate each other more. This is what happens with the soul and God. The agreement has been made. The soul is fully aware of how wonderful her Beloved is, and she is eager to do whatever she can do to make him happy. His Majesty clearly understands the soul's desire to please him, and this does make him happy. So he grants her this mercy: wishing for her to know him more intimately, he arranges for them to meet alone together, as they say, and joins himself with her.

We can compare this union to that kind of exchange because they are both over quickly. There is no more giving and taking. Now the soul has caught a secret glimpse of who this Spouse she is about to accept really is. She could not comprehend with her senses and her faculties in a thousand years what she understands here in the briefest moment of direct connection. Being who he is, the Spouse leaves her more worthy from that one meeting for what is called the joining of hands. The soul finds herself so deeply in love that she would do anything in her power to avoid upsetting the balance of this divine betrothal. But if she becomes careless and allows her affection to drift away from him, she loses everything. This loss is just as extreme as the blessings he had been granting her, which far exceed description.

And so I ask the souls whom God has brought to this juncture not to neglect him now. Remove yourselves from opportunities for error. Even in this advanced state the soul is not quite strong enough to withstand temptation. Later, she will be. In the next dwelling, the engagement between the soul and her God will be complete. For now, their communication is based upon a single tryst, as they say. The spirit of evil will meticulously plan its strategies to combat this betrothal and ruin the marriage. Later, once it sees how completely the soul is surrendered to her Spouse, it doesn't dare make trouble. It knows by experience that if it tries anything, its own loss will be radical and the soul's gain even greater.

I tell you, friends, I have known people who were quite elevated and, having reached this state, still succumbed to the insidious deceit of the spirit of evil. As I have often said, if the spirit of evil is to win over a single soul of this high station it must have to gather together all the forces of the underworld, because the downfall of such a soul includes the downfall of a whole multitude.

The spirit of evil has a lot of experience in this area. Think of how many souls God can draw to himself through a single holy being. The martyrs inspired thousands to praise God. Look at Saint Ursula. What about all the souls that got away from the spirit of evil through the instruments of Saint Dominic and Saint Francis and the founders of other spiritual lineages? Now it's Father Ignatius [of Loyola] who causes the spirit of evil to lose souls. Each of these saints, as we have read, received similar favors from God. All they did was stay strong in their commitment to not jeopardize the divine betrothal through their own unconsciousness.

Oh, my friends! This Beloved of ours is as ready to grant favors to us right now as he was to those others back then. Maybe even more so. There seem to be fewer souls these days who care about receiving his blessing. He needs us. We're too self-absorbed, too attached to our individual rights. What a big mistake we make! May the Beloved in his mercy enlighten us so that we do not fall into such darkness.

There are a couple of things you might wish to ask me at this point. First, if we are prepared to do the will of God and want nothing but to align ourselves with it in everything, how can we be deceived? Next, if we are withdrawn from the world, how can the spirit of evil find us and lead us into danger? We are souls who have cultivated detachment and are intimate with the sacraments. We live, you might say, in the company of angels. We have no other desire than to serve God and please him in everything. Falling off the path would not be so surprising for those who are immersed in the world, you might point out, but for us? I would concede that you are right to ask such a question. The Beloved has been abundantly merciful to us. But when I reflect on the fact that Judas lived among the apostles, was in continuous conversation with Christ himself, and was receiving a direct transmission of the teachings, I realize that our safety as souls is not guaranteed.

What I would answer to your first question is that if the soul held unwaveringly to the will of God she would be in no danger of going astray. But the spirit of evil comes along with its skillful little tricks and, borrowing the colors of good, deceives the soul in all kinds of small ways and seduces her into activities it makes her think are harmless. Little by little it darkens her mind, cools her will, and inflates her ego. Eventually, the spirit of evil succeeds in drawing the soul away from the will of God and toward its own.

Which brings us to your second question. There is no enclosure so securely fenced that the spirit of evil cannot get in. There is no desert so remote that it can't go there. Not only that, but it is quite possible that the reason the Beloved even allows access is so that he can observe the behavior of a soul he has chosen to set up as a light for other souls. If she is going to fall, it's better for it to happen early on rather than later when it can cause harm to many other beings.

We must be diligent. We must continuously ask God in prayer to take us by the hand. We must always bear in mind that if he lets go of us, we may plummet into the abyss. We must remember to question ourselves because false confidence is folly. The important thing is to walk with care and mindfulness, witnessing our own progress in the cultivation of virtue. Are we strengthening or weakening in certain areas? Pay special attention to these issues: love for one another; absence of desire to be thought of as someone special; and the impeccable performance of mundane tasks.

If we are vigilant about these things and ask the Beloved to shed light on them, we will be able to discern the gains and losses we have made. But don't worry too much. God is not going to lightly let a soul who has come so close to him slip into the grip of the spirit of evil. It's not that easy. His Majesty is so reluctant to lose such a soul that he offers her a thousand interior warnings so that no potential harm will be hidden from her.

Let the crux of the matter be this: strive to move forward on the spiritual path. If we make no progress, we should take a good look at ourselves. The spirit of evil may well be trying to impede us, because it simply is not possible that a soul who has come this far would stop growing. Love is never idle, so failure to grow would not be a good sign. A soul who has set out to be the betrothed of God himself, who has become that intimate with His Majesty, who has reached the borders of the land we have been describing, must not lie down and fall back to sleep.

As we begin to explore the sixth dwelling, friends, you will see how he starts to treat those whom he will be taking as his bride. And you will see how little we can do to prepare ourselves for such great blessings, no matter how passionately we serve or patiently we suffer. It could be our Beloved's idea that I have been commanded to write this so that we might forget our trivial worldly concerns and fix our eyes on the true object of our longing. In this way we become aware of his immeasurable mercy as he seems to be absolutely delighted to communicate and reveal himself to some worms. And so, with our gaze one-pointed on his greatness, we rush along on fire with his love.

May he be pleased that I manage to explain something about these difficult things. I know that unless His Majesty and the Holy Spirit move my pen, this will be impossible. If what I have to say does not serve you, I beseech him to keep me from saying anything. His Majesty understands that, to the extent that I know myself, my only desire is to praise him.

Let us rise up to serve such a Lord who even here on earth offers such sweet rewards and inspires us to imagine what he will give to us in heaven, minus the delays and trials and dangers we encounter here on this tempestuous sea. If there wasn't the possibility of losing him or pushing him away, it would be easy to endure this life until the end of the world just so that we could be of service to such a great God and beautiful Beloved.

May it please His Majesty that we be worthy to render him some service, free from the petty errors we always seem to be committing even in doing our good works! Amen.

Sixth Dwelling

Now, with the help of the Holy Spirit, let's take a look at the sixth dwelling. Here the soul is wounded with love for her Spouse and is always looking for space to be alone. In response to her woundedness, she strives to strip away anything that might get in the way of her solitude. From her tryst with the Beloved, the taste of him is so deeply imprinted on the soul that the whole of her desire is to enjoy him all over again. Remember: in this state of prayer nothing can be seen—not in the ordinary sense of seeing, anyway—not even in the imagination.

By now the soul is firmly determined to marry no one but him. Still, the Beloved pays little attention to her yearnings to get on with the wedding. He wants her desire to grow even deeper. He is making the soul pay a high price for this betrothal, since it is such a precious blessing. Even though everything else pales in comparison with this exceedingly great thing, I tell you, friends, the soul has a burning need for some kind of clear token of the promise of her engagement to the Beloved if she is going to be able to stand the waiting.

Oh, God help me! Such radical inner and outer trials the soul must suffer before entering the seventh dwelling!

When I think about it sometimes, I'm afraid that if the soul managed to glimpse what is to come, her feeble nature would undermine her drive to meet the challenges, no matter how alluring the rewards for enduring them might appear to be. This reluctance melts away in the seventh dwelling where the soul finds herself with nothing left to fear and is unconditionally willing to plunge deep into suffering for the sake of God. That's when the soul is so connected to His Majesty that she is able to fortify herself with his nearness. Although not everyone will undergo the trials I am about to speak of, it is unlikely that anyone who tastes the things of heaven in this life will ever be able to avoid earthly strife altogether.

I wasn't going to mention some of these trials, but then I thought it could be a source of comfort to souls facing similar challenges and receiving similar favors from God. When you're going through such strife, everything really does seem hopeless. I'm not going to talk about these hardships in any specific order but rather as they pop into my mind. I'll start with the more petty trials.

A certain person is the target of an uproar being created

by some people she is dealing with and some others she hardly knows and never imagined would even bother to give her a second thought. The gossip goes something like this: "She thinks she's such a saint!" or, "She's falling all over herself to deceive the world and make it seem like other people are missing the mark when in fact they are more spiritual than she is only they don't put on an outward show." It's worth noting, by the way, that she's not putting on any kind of show but just striving to fulfill her station.

People she had believed to be her friends turn on her; they're the ones who take the biggest bite out of her. They regret that this is a soul who has "gone astray" and is obviously "deluded." They lament that she has deceived her spiritual guides and is responsible for an overall decline in virtue. They run to these guides, eager to point this out, citing tragic examples of other souls who have been lost in similar fashion. They come up with a thousand other ridiculous accusations, scoffing at the poor creature the entire time.

I know a certain person so damaged by gossip like this that she didn't think there was a spiritual guide anywhere in the vicinity that would be willing to work with her. The worst part of this kind of hearsay is that it doesn't just blow over quickly; the negative repercussions ripple through the person's whole life. The rumors that this is a person to be avoided at all costs spread out of control.

You may try to reassure me that there are also some people who speak well of such a soul. But oh, friends, how few people there are who will believe the good things they hear compared to the ones who believe all the bad things they are told about souls like us!

Besides, praise is just another trial, even harsher than the ones we've been discussing. The soul sees clearly that if there is anything good in her, it is on loan from God and does not belong to her. Right before she was praised she was noticing how impoverished she feels, how mired in error and unconsciousness. Early on the spiritual journey, at least, praise can be an unbearable burden. As the soul progresses on the path, praise doesn't bother her quite as much.

There are a few reasons for this shift. One, experience demonstrates that people are as quick to make positive judgments as negative ones and so the soul is not inclined to pay much attention to either version. Two, the Beloved has enlightened her enough by now for her to see that anything that is good about her comes not from herself but from His Majesty. This moves her to praise God, and she forgets that she has any connection to this goodness; it is as if it were another person's virtues being extolled. Three, when she sees that other souls have benefited from witnessing the favors God has granted her, she can comfort herself by imagining that God might only be allowing them to mistake her for the source of good so that certain blessings can be transmitted to them. Finally, since the glory of God now matters far more to the soul than her own honor, the temptation with which she used to struggle that made praise so perilous falls away. One to her is fame and blame. If either kind of judgment causes even one soul to praise God, this is a price the soul will gladly pay, come what may.

Although these insights mitigate the great distress the soul feels when she is praised, she still suffers unless she can succeed in ignoring the issue altogether. But for the soul to find herself publicly declared as good without any reason is the most painful trial of all. Once the soul has learned how to stop reacting against approval or recoiling from disapproval, blame will start to sound like sweet music to her ears. This is the truth. Criticism begins to fortify the soul rather than intimidate her. She has already discovered from experience the great benefits to be gained from an attitude of yielding. Rather than view her persecutors as doing something offensive to God, the soul concludes that His Majesty must be allowing this to happen for her own advantage. Since she has reaped the fruits of persecution, a special and very tender love for her detractors grows in her heart. She considers them to be truer friends and more helpful allies than those who speak well of her.

The Lord also has a tendency to send grave ailments. When they are accompanied by intense pain these can be the greatest of all teachers. Intense pain penetrates the soul both on the outside and within and can be so oppressive that she doesn't know what to do with herself. She would trade in this acute suffering for any other version of martyrdom. Fortunately, the intensity of pain doesn't last long. It is said that God doesn't give us more than we can handle, and the first thing he gives us is patience.

I know a certain person who cannot rightfully say that she has been free from physical pain or health problems since that day nearly forty years ago when the Beloved first began to bless her in the ways we have been talking about. It is true that she had not exactly been the most virtuous person in the world up to that point and so at first all the difficulties she had to put up with seemed small in comparison to the consequences she felt she deserved. Others, who have not offended the Beloved quite so much, will be led down a different road. Personally, I would always choose the path of suffering. If this choice was only a matter of emulating our Beloved Jesus Christ, it would be a good enough reason. As it turns out, there are many other advantages.

Oh, but what about the inner suffering? Compared to this, all external challenges are like nothing. If only I could describe how they happen, this distinction would make sense, but I can't.

Let's begin with the torment of working with a spiritual guide who is so inexperienced and so prudent that there is nothing he feels sure about. He's afraid of everything. Everything is cause for doubt. He doesn't know what to make of unconventional experiences. If he perceives any imperfection in the soul who is undergoing these experiences, his doubts become magnified. He presupposes that God only grants such blessings to angels and assumes that since these souls are still in bodies, the whole affair must spring either from the spirit of evil or from mental illness.

Mental illness runs so deep in the world these days, and the spirit of evil takes such terrible advantage of it to cause harm, that spiritual guides are quite correct to be concerned about it. But the poor soul who harbors that same dread and goes to her spiritual guide to try to get some clarity about it only to be condemned by him cannot help but feel deeply disturbed and tormented by his judgment that her extraordinary states are the result of nothing but psychosis or sheer wickedness. Only someone who has struggled with these kinds of self-doubts will know what torture it is.

Another one of the terrible trials the soul must endure is the thought that because of her imperfectly lived life, God is allowing her to be deceived about divine things. While she is in the midst of her altered state, the soul feels fully secure and could never imagine that such sublime gifts could come from any other spirit than God. But since this favor passes quickly, she is plunged immediately back into torment. These heightened states are fleeting, while self-doubt is a constant companion. When her spiritual guide makes an effort to reassure the soul, it calms her—at least for a little while. But when he only adds to her fear with fear of his own, her suffering becomes almost unbearable. It's even worse when those states of exaltation are punctuated by periods of internal aridity. From that place of emptiness it seems to the soul as if she never has been aware of God and never will be. When someone talks about His Majesty, it feels to her that they are referring to someone far, far away.

None of this would matter much except for the fact that it is compounded by her suspicion that she might be misleading her guides by not communicating her experiences clearly enough. She does believe that she has reported every nuance, but she can't seem to console herself with this. Her mind becomes so dark that the soul is incapable of seeing the truth. Her imagination is now her master, and she believes everything it suggests to her.

Our Beloved seems to have given the spirit of evil free rein to test the soul and fool her into thinking that God has forsaken her. The innumerable severe things that wage war inside the soul are so oppressive that I don't know what else to compare the experience to except burning in the fires of the underworld. In the midst of this storm, any sense of consolation is impossible. When she goes to her guide for reassurance, it seems that all that happens is that demons come along to assist him in torturing her even more.

A certain person went to a spiritual guide after one of those heightened states had passed, and she was suffering these kinds of inner doubts. Since the experience was putting her through such agony, he concluded that what had happened to her must have been a very bad thing. He told her to let him know whenever she started to go into one of these states, and he would see what he could do. But her suffering was so intense, he decided that it was out of his hands. If a person in this predicament who knew how to read perfectly well were to pick up an ordinary romance novel at this time, she would be able to make no more sense of it than if she didn't know a single letter of the alphabet; that's how shut down the intellect has become.

Ultimately, there is no remedy for this tempest but to wait for the mercy of God. At the most unexpected time, with a single word or a random circumstance, he will so swiftly calm the storm that it will seem as if there had never been a single cloud in the sky of the soul. She will be flooded with the sunshine of solace. Like someone who has escaped a treacherous battle and emerged victorious, the soul comes out praising the Lord, since she knows he is the one who fought for victory. In fact, she notices that all of the weapons she would have used to defend herself are in the hands of her foes. She becomes brutally aware of her insignificance and realizes how little we would be able to do to help ourselves if the Beloved ever decided to abandon us.

It doesn't require a great deal of reflection to understand this. The soul has experienced it. She has suffered, seeing herself as totally powerless. She has grasped her own nothingness. Despite all this torment, the soul does not do a thing that might possibly offend God, nor would she ever consider causing him offense for anything on earth. Still, what grace there is in this state lies so deeply buried that not even a tiny spark can be perceived. The soul begins to doubt that she has ever really loved God. It feels to the soul as if any good she may have ever done or any blessing His Majesty has ever granted her was only some kind of dream or delusion. All she knows for sure is that she has made many mistakes.

Oh, Jesus Christ! How sad it is to see a soul so vulnerable, how worthless any earthly comfort! Do not think for a minute, friends, that the wealthy have any freer access to a remedy for their brokenness than you do. No, no. It's like offering all the delights of the world to a man condemned to die. Would knowledge of these mundane comforts alleviate his suffering one iota? No; in fact it would only intensify the torment. The suffering comes from above, and it is from above that we must draw comfort. Before we can progress on the path, our great God wants us to know that he is king and we are humble creatures.

Well, what is the poor soul to do when this torment goes on and on? When she prays, it's as if she weren't even engaging in prayer, for all the consolation it gives her. No consolation can filter into the interior of the soul. Vocal prayer sounds meaningless to the soul in this state even when she is in the midst of reciting it. Mental prayer is absolutely impossible for this soul because her faculties are not functioning. Solitude is torture but the company of others is worse. It's dangerous for her to be alone, but she can't bear to have anyone speak to her, either. And so, though she tries hard to cover up her misery, she goes around gloomy and irritable and everybody notices it.

How could she ever begin to say what's bothering her? These problems are spiritual afflictions and they are unnameable. Although there is no cure for such a malady, the best medicine for achieving temporary relief is to engage in external work and service and to hope in the mercy of God who never fails those who hope in him. May he be forever blessed. Amen.

There are other less common trials imposed by evil spirits, but they are superficial and not worth mentioning. Whatever trouble these spirits stir up, they cannot disable the faculties or disturb the interior of the soul. After all, they can do no more than what the Beloved allows them to do. As long as you don't lose your mind, all outer strife is inconsequential.

Then there are inner challenges the soul encounters in this dwelling arising from different kinds of prayer and blessings the Beloved bestows. Some of these blessings impact the body and cause even more severe pain than the kind we've been talking about. But they do not qualify as trials since they are actually divine favors, and the soul recognizes them to be such and can hardly even believe that she deserves them.

This intensity of strife pays the soul's passage to the seventh dwelling. It would be impossible to speak of the true nature of the suffering to come; it is of a much higher order than what we've explored so far. If I've been unsuccessful in conveying anything of these lower trials, think about how much less I will be able to communicate about this more rarefied kind! May the Lord help me in everything I do through the excellence of his Son. Amen.

It may seem like we have left our little butterfly behind, but we haven't. Uplifted by these trials, she flies higher and higher.

So now let's start looking at how the Beloved is dealing with the soul during this time. Before fully uniting himself with her, he fills her with burning desire for him. He does this in such a delicate way that the soul doesn't understand where her longing comes from, nor could I successfully explain it except to those of you who already know from experience what I'm saying. These impulses rise from so deep inside the soul and are so subtle and refined that I can't find a fitting metaphor to describe them.

This experience is far different from anything we can

taste in the world. It is even different from the spiritual delights we have talked about so far. Often when a seeker is distracted and forgets about God, he will awaken her. His gesture is as swift as a shooting star and as resounding as a thunderbolt. Although his call is soundless, the soul is left with no doubt that he is calling her. This is so clear to her that sometimes, especially at the beginning, she may tremble and whimper without any obvious cause for her pain. She feels that she has been wounded in the sweetest way, but she can't figure out how it happened or who inflicted it. All she knows is that the wound is something precious and she doesn't ever want to recover!

The soul cannot restrain herself from lamenting to her Spouse with words of love. She may even cry out loud. She knows that he is with her, but he refuses to reveal himself in such a way that she can actually enjoy him. The pain is intense, but it is exquisite and delightful. Even if the soul chose not to go through this, there is nothing she could do to avoid it. But she would never wish for the wound to go away. This kind of agony is much more satisfying to the soul than the sweet and painless absorption of the Prayer of Quiet.

I am struggling, friends, to explain this movement of love to you. I don't know how. It seems like a contradiction to say that the Beloved makes it clear to the soul that he is with her and at the same time gives her an equally clear sign that he is calling her. His whistle is so penetrating that she can't help but hear it. The Spouse, who is in the seventh dwelling, summons the soul wordlessly. The inhabitants of the other dwellings, which are the faculties of sense and reason and the imagination, do not dare to stir.

Oh, my powerful God! How great are your secrets and how different they are from anything we are used to seeing or thinking about in the mundane world! These favors are ineffable, though they don't even compare with the most exalted blessings you bestow on souls.

This action of love is so potent that the soul melts with desire. And yet she can't think of what to ask for since she is clearly feeling the presence of her God. If she knows that he is with her, you will ask me, then what is it that she wants and what is causing her such distress? What greater blessing could she possibly desire? I don't know. What I do know is that the pain penetrates the very depths of the soul. And so, when he who has wounded her withdraws his arrow, it seems like God is drawing out her innermost depths, in proportion to the love she feels for him.

I was just thinking that it is as if a spark leaps from the hearth that is my God and presses into the soul, smoldering, but not quite hot enough to set her on fire. The mere touch of an ember leaves the soul with a delicious burning, an exquisite pain. This is the best comparison I seem to be able to come up with. And this exquisite pain-that-is-not-pain isn't continuous but may last for a long time or may pass very quickly. It depends on how the Beloved wishes to transmit it. There is nothing we can do through our own efforts to procure it. It comes and goes; it is never permanent. That's why it doesn't light the soul on fire. Just when she is on the verge of bursting into flame, the fire goes out, leaving the soul yearning to suffer that loving pain all over again.

There is no reason to think that this experience has anything to do with our physical nature, or is an effect of depression, or some trick being played by the spirit of evil, or mere delusion. It is clear to the soul that this inner burning comes from the place where the Lord who is unchanging dwells. It isn't like any other devotional episode when we might doubt ourselves simply based on the intensity of absorption in joy that we experience. Here the faculties are not absorbed but are vigilantly monitoring what is going on, wondering what it's all about. They can't get in the way of what's happening. They can neither increase the delicious pain nor take it away.

If the Beloved has ever granted you this favor, you will know it when you read this, and you should offer him thanks from the bottom of your heart. You do not have to worry that you have been deceived. Concern yourself instead with expressing sufficient gratitude for such a generous boon. Strive to serve God and improve the whole of your life. Then you will find yourself to be the recipient of greater and greater blessings. A certain person who was granted this favor and enjoyed it for a number of years was so satisfied by it that she would have gladly suffered an equal duration of trials to give back to God for such a great gift. May he be blessed forever. Amen.

Are you wondering why we feel more secure in this pain than we do with other favors? I think there are a few reasons for this. One, the spirit of evil could never transmit such sweet suffering. True, it may give the soul counterfeit bliss, which it tries to make her think of as spiritual. But it does not have the power to unite pain—and so much of it!—with the spiritual quietude and joy of the soul. The power of evil is external and superficial. The pain it causes is never accompanied by peace or delight but always stirs restlessness and contention. Two, this sweet storm comes from a realm where evil has no authority. Three, the soul is left with wondrous benefits from her encounter with this fire. The most essential of these is the determination that fills her to suffer for the sake of God, the desire to withstand many trials, and the impulse to withdraw from worldly concerns.

It's obvious that this favor is no mere whim. Although at other times she strives to experience feelings like this, she cannot fake this one. It is such a palpable thing that it cannot be mistaken for a figment of the imagination. Such an experience transcends all doubt, so if any doubt remains it is evidence that what the soul has experienced is not the real thing. We perceive a genuine favor as clearly as we hear a loud voice. There is no way it can be caused by mental imbalance, either. The delusions derived from mental imbalance play out on the stage of the imagination. This is a thing that springs from the innermost part of the soul.

Now, it could be that I'm mistaken about all this, but until I hear otherwise from someone who understands the matter, I will hold to my opinion. I know a certain person who was terribly afraid of being deceived in that way but who never had any fear of this kind of prayer.

Our Beloved has other ways of awakening the soul, as well. Unexpectedly—while she is praying aloud, for instance, and not thinking about interior things—she seems to suddenly burst into sweet flame. It is as if a powerful fragrance had engulfed her and spread through all her senses, though this is a phenomenon that utterly transcends the sensual. The entire purpose of this feeling is to let the soul know that her Spouse is with her. The soul is overcome by a delicious desire to enjoy him. She is ready to make intense acts of love and to sing the praises of her Beloved.

This favor rises from the deepest chamber of the soul, but there is nothing here that causes distress, nor are the soul's desires to enjoy the Beloved at all painful. This is usually how the soul experiences the fire of love, anyway. Remember: there is no reason to be afraid; rather, you should surrender and receive this blessing with gratitude.

. 3 .

God has some other ways of awakening the soul. Here's one that may well be an even greater favor than the blessings we've talked about so far, but it can also be more dangerous. That's why I'm going to take some time to describe it more carefully.

The blessing I am talking about takes the form of a spiritual voice—a kind of auditory vision. There are different kinds of spiritual voices. Some seem to come from outside the soul, others from her innermost depths. Some filter down from her own highest part and others are so exterior that the soul seems to hear them with her ears, as if a physical voice had spoken them. Sometimes a spiritual voice can be nothing but the figment of a feeble imagination or an artifact of mental imbalance.

In my opinion, we shouldn't pay too much attention to these delusional manifestations, even if the people reporting on them claim to be understanding everything they're hearing. But neither should we upset them by telling them that their spiritual voices come from the spirit of evil. We should listen to them as we would listen to sick people: with compassion. You might tactfully advise them not to cling to these experiences but to let them go, reminding them that spiritual voices have little to do with serving God. Mention that the spirit of evil has deceived many souls in this way but reassure them that you are not implying that they themselves are suffering from such deception. This counsel should be offered gently, so as not to aggravate the imbalance. If we suggest that the person is crazy, she will just grow more agitated, insisting that she hears what she hears and knows what she knows. That's how convinced she is herself.

The best thing to do with people in a delusional state is to minimize their access to contemplative practice for a while and discourage them from attaching any importance to spiritual voices. The spirit of evil tends to take advantage of people who suffer from mental illness and causes harm not only to them but to the people around them. Still, whether the person reporting these experiences is sick or healthy, it's always wise to carefully question their spirit until the truth becomes clear.

I say that early on the journey it is always better to let spiritual voices go. If the experience does come from God, detaching from it will help us evolve. When we are tested, we grow. Yet, while this is absolutely true, we should never make a soul feel badly about her experience because she truly can't help it; the spiritual voices just come.

Remember: spiritual voices may come from God, from the spirit of evil, or from our own imagination. With the Beloved's help, I hope I can manage now to describe the signs that indicate the source of the spiritual voices and how they differ from each other and whether or not they are dangerous. Many people who practice prayer hear things. If you refuse to take them seriously, friends, I want you to know that you are doing right. It doesn't matter if these things seem to be spoken just for you, offering consolation for some particular disturbance or advice about a specific fault of yours. It doesn't matter who is telling you these things or if they are delusions. Even when the spiritual voices do come from God, I warn you: don't think that you will be any better because of them.

After all, didn't Christ talk a lot to the Pharisees? All good comes from what we do with what we hear. Unless these messages are in harmony with revealed truth, dismiss them as swiftly as you would words spoken by the spirit of evil itself. If they arise from your own weak imagination, it's best to treat them as temptations threatening your faith and to resist them. Once they hold no power over you, they will just go away by themselves.

Whether these spiritual voices come from within, from above, or from outside of the soul has nothing to do with the question of whether their source is divine. Here are the clearest indications, in my opinion, that a spiritual voice comes from God.

The first and truest sign is the power and authority they bear. That which is revealed in words is manifested in works. Let me try to explain this better. Say the soul finds herself immersed in tribulations and inner disquiet. Her mind feels dark and her spirit arid. It seems to the soul that if all the wise men in the world were to line up and give her reasons why everything is all right, they could not alleviate her pain one iota, no matter how hard they tried. Alone in prayer, she hears a single phrase: "Be not troubled," and all at once she is calm. A great light shines upon her and lifts away her distress. Just like that!

Or maybe the soul is upset because after confiding in her spiritual guide or someone else about an inner experience they tell her that she is being terrorized by an evil energy. Then she hears a voice inside of her: "It is I, fear not," and her fear falls away completely. She is so deeply comforted that she believes no one could ever make her feel otherwise.

Maybe she is overly concerned with certain pressing business matters, apprehensive about how they will turn out. With her inner ear, she hears that she should be calm, that all will be well. Her confidence is instantly renewed, and she is free from worry. We could think of many more examples.

The second sign that a spiritual voice comes from God is

the great quietude left in the soul. She lingers in peaceful recollection and devotion. And yet at the same time she is ready to burst into song praising God. They say that in this dwelling it is not God who speaks directly to the soul but an angel. Oh, Beloved! If a word spoken through one of your messengers has such power, what power will you leave in a soul who is connected to you with ribbons of love and to whom, with love-ribbons, you are connected?

The third sign is that the words do not fade from the memory for a very long time; some stay forever. We may forget the things that men say, even if the people speaking them are important and educated or what they are saying has some significant bearing on our future. But these words do not burn themselves into our memory and we do not believe in them as fully as we do in these divine spiritual voices. These inner messages may seem to be impossible and our minds may balk, doubting they could ever happen, but the certainty inside the soul is unconditional. Maybe everything seems to be opposite to what the soul understood in her spiritual voice. Maybe years go by like this, but she never loses her unshakable faith that God will find other ways than the ways known by men, and in the end what he has said will come to pass. And it does.

The soul still suffers when she encounters all these detours and delays. Some time may have passed since she first heard the divine words. The inner effects of the message and the soul's certainty about it may have faded. Doubts arise. The soul starts to wonder if the whole thing may have come from her own imagination or, worse, from the spirit of evil. But these clouds of doubt blow over and once again the soul would stand up and die for her truth. Still, I say it is the spirit of evil that stirs up the imagination to afflict and intimidate the soul and get her to doubt herself. This is especially true if the spiritual voice has something to do with a business matter that, when implemented, would bring many blessings to many souls or create good works that would honor and serve God but involve significant challenges. What will the spirit of evil not do to shake the soul's faith and damage the cause by making her wonder if God actually does have the power to do things that are incomprehensible to our intellects?

In spite of all these struggles—where people she confides in may pronounce her a fool for believing in these spiritual voices and negative circumstances tempt her to conclude that they must not be true—still there remains a spark of living certainty inside the soul. I don't know where it comes from. But it assures her that no matter how hard she tried, the soul could never kill this spark, which continues to shine even when all other hopes are dead. In the end, the word of the Lord is fulfilled. The soul is so overjoyed that she would like nothing but to praise His Majesty forever and praise him yet again because what he said would be has come to be.

I don't know why it means so much to the soul that these words turn out to be true. If the soul herself were caught in a web of her own lies, I doubt she would be so anxious to see them verified. All she can do is repeat what she heard. A certain person has thought about this countless times, recalling how Jonah feared that Nineveh would not ever be destroyed.

Ultimately, since these spiritual voices come from the spirit of God, it is right for the soul to hold to her faith that his words will come true, because God is Supreme Truth. And so when, after innumerable circuitous paths and difficult circumstances, God's word is fulfilled, the happiness of the soul is boundless. She would rather bear a thousand unbearable trials than discover that what she was certain the Beloved told her turns out not to be true. Not everybody is this weak. Maybe I shouldn't even refer to it as a weakness, because I find that I cannot condemn this need as being a bad thing.

When spiritual voices arise from the imagination, none of these signs present themselves. The soul lacks certainty, peace, and interior delight. Some people have a weak constitution or a feeble imagination. I know a few people who, while profoundly absorbed in the Prayer of Quiet, have dropped into a spiritual sleep and that's when these kinds of spiritual voices have come to them. I'm not sure what the cause is, but while deep in recollection they slip out of themselves and become unconscious of everything external and all their senses shut down. They may feel like they are asleep and dreaming, and this is probably the case. What they hear and even what they see seems to be coming from God, but they are only dreams. It also happens sometimes that while they are beseeching God for something with great love, they convince themselves that voices are telling them exactly what they want to hear. Yet anyone who has had any experience of the kind of spiritual voices that come from God will not be fooled by those that arise from the imagination.

There is more to fear in the spiritual voices that come from the spirit of evil. But if the spiritual voices carry the signs we've been talking about, you can be sure that they come from God. What if a spiritual voice seems to require that some action be taken regarding something serious about yourself or impacting a third party? You should never consider yourself to be so powerful that you act or even think about acting without consulting a wise and cautious guide whose primary purpose is to serve God. This is true even if you start understanding the spiritual voice better and better and are absolutely clear that it comes from God.

It is His Majesty's will that the soul seek guidance. Doing so doesn't mean that she is failing to do what he has told her. Remember when he said to put our spiritual teachers in his place, knowing that true teachers speak in a sacred way? Let these words give us courage when matters are difficult. As soon as he is ready, the Beloved will let our guide know that the spiritual voice comes from his spirit. If he does not, we are released from obligation and so are they. I consider it to be very dangerous to cling to your own opinion in these things. And so I warn you, friends, in the name of our Beloved, do not neglect to seek wise counsel.

There is another way the Beloved speaks to the soul that I know with absolute certainty to be authentic. Sometimes he communicates through a kind of intellectual vision. I will explain this in more detail later. For now what I can tell you is that this transmission is deeply intimate. The words the Beloved himself speaks are absolutely clear, even though he speaks them secretly. In light of the effects produced by this vision, the soul understands perfectly what she is being told and, when she reflects carefully on it, she has no doubts about its veracity. She can be sure that the spiritual voice comes neither from the spirit of evil nor from her own imagination. There are a few good reasons for her confidence.

One, a genuine spiritual voice is so clear that the soul remembers every word, as well as the tone of voice in which it was spoken, and if a single syllable was missing she notices it. When a spiritual voice is conjured up by the imagination, the voice may be fuzzy and the language indistinct, like something overheard when you are half-asleep.

Two, frequently the soul hadn't even been thinking about the things she hears in the spiritual voice. The transmission often comes unexpectedly, maybe even in the middle of a conversation. Sometimes it does refer directly to a passing thought she had or to something the soul had been pondering more deeply at an earlier time. But it often has to do with a future the soul never believed could or would happen. The imagination can't just make up things that never crossed the mind! The soul could not be deceived about things that she never desired or wished for or even imagined, could she?

Three, in a false spiritual voice her imagination composes bit by bit what the soul wants to hear. In a real one, she hears truth.

Four, the words are received differently. In an authentic spiritual voice, the mind grasps truth far more profoundly and with much greater immediacy than the intellect could ever present on its own.

Five, the truth that is conveyed to the soul on the wings of words simultaneously transcends all words. I'll never be able to explain this! But I will try to say more about this special mode of understanding later. It's an exquisite and subtle thing and cause for praising our Lord.

I know a certain person who has suffered many doubts about these different kinds of spiritual voices and has had a difficult time understanding herself. I'm sure there are others like her. The Beloved has often granted her this kind of favor, and I know that she has considered it carefully. In the beginning she was plagued by the doubt that she had imagined the whole thing. It's easy to spot spiritual voices that come from the spirit of evil, though it employs insidious tricks to mimic the spirit of light. The spirit of evil will enunciate as clearly as the spirit of truth so the meaning cannot be misunderstood, but it won't be able to counterfeit the holy effects that divine spiritual voices have on the soul or leave that peace and light inside her. It yields nothing but restlessness and turmoil. If the soul remains humble and still, no matter what the spiritual voice tells her to do, the spirit of evil can do her no harm.

What about when the spiritual voices bring gifts and consolations from the Beloved? Then the soul must look deeply inside herself to see if this makes her think that she is better than other people. The sweeter the words spoken to her, the greater should be her confusion. If this does not happen, the spirit is not from God. One thing is for sure: the higher the favor granted by God, the less the soul thinks of herself, the deeper her awareness of her own imperfection grows, and the more forgetful she becomes of personal profit. Her will and memory pursue the honor of God with unwavering intensity, and she walks with trepidation so as not to deviate from his will. She is sure that she deserves none of the wondrous favors arising from prayer but only punishment for her unconsciousness.

Since divine blessings yield these humbling effects, the soul does not need to be afraid but can rest in confidence that the mercy of the Lord who is faithful will not allow the spirit of evil to deceive her. Although it is always wise to step carefully through these matters.

It could be that those whom the Beloved does not lead along this path will think that souls who do receive spiritual voices ought to categorically refuse to listen to the words they hear. Maybe they think that since the words are heard with an inner sense the person should simply distract herself in such a way that she blocks them out. They may insist that this is the only way for such souls to avoid danger.

My answer to this: it's impossible. I'm not talking here about imaginary spiritual voices. If these spiritual voices were mere figments of the soul's imagination, they could be cured by detaching from her desires for certain spiritual phenomena and ignoring her own imaginings. When the spiritual voices come from God, there is no remedy. The very spirit who is speaking halts all other thoughts and compels the soul to pay exclusive attention to what he is saying to her. I truly believe that it is more likely for a person with excellent hearing not to hear someone saying something in a very loud voice than it would be for the soul not to apprehend her God in this way.

In the case of the person not hearing the loud voice, he could turn away and tune the speaker out, focusing his attention elsewhere. But in a divine spiritual voice, the soul has nowhere to go. There are no ears to plug up and no power to refrain from thought. For he who was able to stop the sun (at the request of Joshua, I think it was) can call a halt to the faculties and all the inner functionings of the soul so that she clearly sees that another lord, greater than herself, governs the castle. This calls forth deep devotion and humility from the soul.

So, no, there is no cure for this kind of spiritual voice.

May His Divine Majesty teach us to fix our eyes on him alone and forget ourselves. Amen. And may it please God that I have managed to explain what I set out to explain, and may it be of some help to any of you who have experienced these spiritual voices.

What serenity can our poor little butterfly find amid all these trials? Suffering increases her desire to enjoy the Beloved. His Majesty understands our fragility. Through these challenges he gives the soul the strength and courage she needs to unite herself with so great a being and take him for her Spouse.

You will laugh and call it ridiculous when I speak of courage. After all, what woman, no matter how modest, wouldn't have the courage to marry the king? This may not be the case with earthly royalty, but I tell you, more bravery than you might think is required to unite with the king of heaven. Our nature is timid and weak in contrast with something so great. I'm sure that union would be impossible unless God himself gave us the strength to meet him, no matter how clearly we saw the benefits of becoming one with him.

Now you will see what His Majesty does to consummate the engagement. This is what is happening, as I understand it, when he gives the soul raptures, which carry her out beyond her senses. If the soul were to remain connected to her senses and then see herself so close to such magnificence, she might die. Please understand that I am talking about genuine raptures and not the tendencies we women have to turn everything into an ecstatic moment. Remember, there are some people so sensitive that the Prayer of Quiet is enough to kill them!

Through conversations I've had with spiritual people, I have come to understand various kinds of raptures, and I'd like to explore them now. In one kind of rapture, the soul isn't even engaged in prayer, and suddenly she is struck by some word she remembers or hears spoken about God. It seems that His Majesty is moved by compassion when he witnesses the suffering of the soul who has yearned so long for him. He makes that spark burst into flame so that the soul burns up entirely and then, like the phoenix, is reborn. Through her devotion and his grace, all her errors are forgiven. Once she is purified in this way, the Beloved joins her with himself in a manner that only the two of them can understand. Even the soul herself cannot understand it in any kind of sense that she can explain afterwards. But her inner knowing is pristine. This is not an experience like a fit or fainting where nothing is perceived either on the outside or within.

In fact, as I understand it, the soul has never before been so fully awake to the things of God or had such clear-light knowledge of His Majesty. This may sound impossible to you. If the faculties and the senses are so completely absorbed that we can call them dead, how can the soul understand the secret? I don't know. Nor, perhaps, does any creature know! Only the Creator himself understands these things. I can't explain most of the other matters that take place in this state, either, where the door between both of the final dwellings is open and the two places are melded. Since there are truths in the last dwelling that are not revealed to those who haven't yet reached it, I thought I should delineate them.

When the soul is in this state of suspension, the Beloved likes to show her some secret things, heavenly mysteries and imaginative visions. She is able to describe them afterwards only because they are so firmly pressed into her memory that she could never forget them. But when the visions are transcendental, they transcend all concepts, and the soul doesn't have any idea how to speak of them. The visions that come at times like these are so sublime that it simply isn't appropriate for those who live on this earth to apprehend them in such a way that they can be conveyed with words. Still, when the soul regains possession of her senses, there are many things she can say about these visions.

Well, now you will ask me, if the soul doesn't remember the divine favors the Beloved grants her in this state, what use are they? Oh, friends, their greatness cannot be exaggerated! Even though these blessings are ineffable, they are inscribed in the innermost part of the soul and she never, ever forgets them.

But, you will ask me, if there are no images and the faculties cannot comprehend anything, how can the visions be retained? I don't understand this, either. What I do know is that there are truths about the greatness of God that are so firmly planted in the garden of the soul that even if she didn't have faith dictating who he is and compelling her to believe that he is God, the soul would adore him as God from that moment forward.

The soul becomes like Jacob, who believed the instant he saw the ladder. There must have been other secrets Jacob understood but was incapable of describing. Simply seeing a ladder with angels ascending and descending would not have been sufficient to reveal to him the meaning of such profound mysteries unless he had been given a deeper inner light. I'm not entirely sure I'm looking at this right because, though I've heard the story, I don't always remember things accurately.

Moses didn't know how to describe every single thing that he saw in the burning bush. He could only hold onto the details that God wished for him to transmit. Still, if God had not revealed these secrets to his soul and instilled within him the absolute certainty that they came from God, Moses would not have taken upon himself such arduous trials. But he must have learned such wondrous things among the thorns of the bush that they gave him the courage he needed to do what he did for the people of Israel.

So, friends, we don't need to look for reasons to justify the hidden things of God. Since we believe he is omnipotent, we must see that it is impossible for undeveloped worms like us with our limited powers to understand his greatness. Let us praise him with all our hearts for being pleased to allow us to understand a part of it.

I've been trying to come up with a decent metaphor to describe these things, and I don't think there are any that really fit. But let's try this one: you enter the private chamber of a king or a dignitary. Maybe it's the secret place where the treasure of the kingdom is stored. There you discover an infinite variety of glassware and crockery and other beautiful objects arranged in such a way that you can see them all as soon as you walk in.

I was once brought into a room like this at the Duchess of Alba's house. Due to the insistence of this great lady's invitation, my superior ordered me to spend a few days there in the midst of a cross-country journey. When I went into that room, I was amazed by all those things, and I wondered what use there was for such a vast array. Then I realized that seeing so many different kinds of objects could inspire one to praise the Lord.

I find myself amazed now by how I've been able to borrow that experience to help me with my present purpose! Although I stood in that place for a while, there was so much to see that I couldn't remember it all. In fact, I've forgotten so much of it that it's as if I had never even been there. I can say that I remember having seen these things as a whole, but I couldn't tell you how individual items were crafted or even what materials they were made of.

That's what it's like with this divine favor. The soul becomes one with God. She is picked up and placed in the innermost chamber of the highest heaven. Since it is clear that God abides within us, then we must have these dwelling places inside our own souls. The Beloved doesn't want the soul to see these secrets every single time she goes into an ecstasy. And sometimes she is simply so absorbed in enjoying him that this sublime blessing is enough for her. But sometimes he is pleased for her to disconnect from her absorption a little so that she can see what's around her in this special room. After she returns to herself, the soul is able to remember the revelation of the precious treasures she saw. She can't describe any of them, though. Her nature prevents her from apprehending any more of the supernatural bounty than God wills for her to take in.

It might sound to you like I am admitting that the soul is actually perceiving something and is having some kind of imaginative vision. I'm not saying that. This is not a vision that includes images; it is an intellectual vision. The problem is that I am uneducated, and I lack the sophistication to explain things properly. If I have succeeded in saying anything worthwhile about prayer so far, you can be sure that I'm not the one who has said it!

It is my belief that if the soul who goes through these

raptures never understands any of the secrets, then the raptures are not coming from God but rather from some weakness in that person's own nature. There are people so fragile that any spiritual force will overwhelm their natural powers, and they will be plunged into absorption. These experiences have nothing to do with holy rapture. In a true ecstasy—believe me—God carries the whole soul off for himself. And then, as you would expect when someone is made part of a family, he starts showing her around the kingdom that has become hers by marriage. Maybe only a small part is revealed at this time, but everything that there is in this great God is magnificent. The Beloved will not allow his lover to be disturbed by anyone—not the faculties, not the senses—and so he commands that the doors to all the other dwelling places be shut. Only the passage to his chamber remains open so that the soul can enter.

Blessed be so much mercy! Woe be to those who have chosen not to walk through that door and so have lost their Beloved!

Oh, my friends! All that we leave behind is mere nothingness. All that we do or could ever do for a God so willing to communicate himself to a humble worm: nothingness. If we have any hope of enjoying such blessings in this life, what are we doing? What are we waiting for? What could possibly constitute sufficient reason for us to stop looking for this Beloved even for a moment with the same one-pointedness with which the bride searched for him in the streets and squares? What a travesty everything in the world is if it doesn't help lead us to God! I don't care if all imaginable earthly delights were piled up before us and would last forever. It is nothing but disgusting garbage compared to these treasures that will endure without end. And these blessings themselves do not compare with the sheer grace of having as our own the Lord of all the treasures of heaven and earth!

Oh, human blindness! How long, how long until this dust is removed from our eyes? Even though it may hardly seem bad enough to blind us completely, I see some motes and particles that, if allowed to accumulate, could do us great harm. For the love of God, friends, let us benefit from our faults and learn from our mistakes. Then our imperfections will clear our vision, as the mud healed the blind man when our Spouse placed it on his eyes. By witnessing our transgressions we are able to surrender ourselves to the mercy of our Beloved so that he can draw goodness out of our negativity and we can be even more pleasing to him.

I have digressed a great deal without realizing it. Please excuse me, friends, and believe me that now that I have come upon this greatness of God (come to the place where I'm ready to write about it, I mean), I can't help feeling very sorry to see all that we lose through our own unconsciousness. While it is true that the Beloved grants his blessings to whomever he wills, His Majesty would gladly give them to us all if only we loved him as he loves us. He desires nothing but to have souls to give them to! His riches are not diminished one bit by giving them away.

Getting back to what I was saying: the Spouse orders the

doors of all other rooms to be closed, and the entrance to the castle itself, and the courtyard, too. When he carries off the soul, he takes her breath away. Even if the other senses linger for a while, the person cannot possibly speak. Sometimes everything is stolen away at once, and the hands and limbs grow so still and cold that it appears as if there were no life left in the body. Sometimes you can't be sure the person is still breathing. This kind of intensity only lasts for a short period at any one time. When the profound suspension lifts a little, it seems that the body slowly comes back to itself and is nourished only to die all over again and give fuller life to the soul. Total ecstasy does not last too long.

But even after the rapture has passed, the will remains so deeply absorbed and the mind so transported that for days the mind is incapable of understanding anything that does not awaken the will to love. And the will is so wide awake to love that it is fast asleep to all attachments to any creature.

Oh, what bewilderment the soul feels when she returns to herself! How intense are her desires that God use her however he wants! The soul would gladly have a thousand lives to be able to give them all to God. She wishes that everything on earth could be a tongue to help her praise him. She has this strong urge to sacrifice herself for him, but the power of her love makes the soul feel that what she has to offer is insignificant. She realizes that the martyrs didn't accomplish much in enduring the torments they endured because with the help of our Beloved such suffering is easy. Still our souls complain to

His Majesty when he deprives us of the opportunity to offer ourselves as a sacrifice to him.

The soul prefers divine favors that are granted to her in secret. When they are given in front of others she becomes so embarrassed that worry and shame over who saw it and what they might think about it detracts to some extent from the blessing she is enjoying. Knowing the malice of the world, she understands that people might not recognize the experience for what it is and instead of serving as an opportunity for praising the Lord, it will instead be the occasion for harsh judgments. Although the soul cannot control this self-consciousness, it seems to me to indicate a certain lack of humility. If this soul truly wishes to be humble, then who cares what other people think?

I know a certain person who was suffering in this way and she heard our Beloved say to her, "Don't be afflicted. They will either praise me or criticize you. Either way, you win." I found out later that this person had been deeply consoled and cheered up by these words, and so I've written them down here in case any of you might be suffering such distress.

It seems that our Beloved wants everyone to know that this soul is now his and that no one should touch her. People are welcome to attack the body, the honor, or the possessions of the lover of God because she will use all of these things as further opportunities for glorifying His Majesty. But to attack the soul: absolutely not! Unless the soul purposely (and with extreme stupidity) pulls away from her Beloved, he will protect her from all the world and even from the underworld.

I don't know if I've been able to explain anything substantial about the nature of rapture. It's impossible to describe. But I doubt we've lost anything by trying. It's important to see the differences between real raptures and false ones. When I say "false raptures," I don't mean that the person having the rapture is faking it to deceive us, but rather the person having the rapture is being deceived herself. Since the signs and effects of false raptures are not in harmony with authentic blessings, true raptures may end up getting discredited. Then, when the Beloved grants the real thing later, no one believes it!

May he be blessed and praised forever. Amen. Amen.

.5.

There is another kind of rapture God gives to the soul. I call it a flight of the spirit. In essence, it's the same as the other kind of raptures, but the soul experiences it very differently inside herself. Suddenly, the soul will become aware of a movement so swift that it seems as if her spirit were being whisked away. The sheer speed of this movement is terrifying—at least in the beginning. This is why I say that the soul who is granted this favor must be brave. She must also have faith and confidence, and she must be fully surrendered to our Beloved so that he can do whatever he wants with her. It's rather disturbing, to say the least, for a person in complete control of her senses to be suddenly carried off like that. I have heard of certain people whose bodies were even raised up with their spirits! Do you think that the soul has any idea what is going on, where she's headed, or who is doing this to her or how? No. When this rapid movement first lifts the soul away, she cannot know for sure that the rapture comes from God.

Well, does the soul have any power to resist this transport? None whatsoever. In fact, resistance only makes matters worse. I watched this happen with a certain person. It seems that it was God's will for a soul who had so often and unconditionally placed herself in his hands to be reminded that she was no longer the director of her own program, and he wrested the controls away from her with a force that was difficult to ignore. Have you ever noticed how a blade of straw is folded into a piece of amber? This particular soul remembered that the safest thing is to make a virtue of necessity. She abandoned herself into the hands of the One who is all-powerful. Yes, the soul is like a straw, and it is no easier for a strong man to pick up a straw than it is for this great Giant of ours to carry away the spirit.

Was it in the fourth dwelling that we talked about the water trough? I don't remember exactly. What I do know is that basin filled gently and quietly. I mean, it filled without any perceptible movement. But now our great God—who controls the water at its source and doesn't allow the ocean to move beyond its boundaries—releases the spring from which the water in this basin flows. With a powerful thrust, an immense wave rises up so forcefully that the little ship of the spirit is lifted high. Can a boat keep a tidal wave from depositing her wherever it will? It cannot. Does a captain or his crew have authority over a storm at sea? They do not. The interior part of the soul has even less power to stop wherever she happens to feel like stopping. She can't make her senses or faculties do anything other than what they are being commanded to do. The exterior senses are oblivious to the whole thing.

Really, friends, as I reflect on how the tremendous power of this great Emperor is manifested here, I am amazed just writing about it. How much more intense will be the astonishment felt by the person who gets to experience it firsthand? It is my belief that if His Majesty were to reveal himself to souls who are going astray in this world in the way that he reveals himself to these others, then, from fear, even if not from love, they would not dare to offend him. Think of how much greater will be the motivation of souls moved in that sublime way to strive with all their might to honor the Beloved!

For love of him, friends, I beg you, those of you the Beloved has blessed with these and similar favors, not to become careless. Don't just sit back and take them in. Bear in mind that she who receives much has much to give back.

This thought in itself is a scary one. If the Beloved did not give the soul courage, she would be perpetually distressed. That's because whenever she considers all that His Majesty does for her and then turns back to look at herself, she can't help but notice how little she gives in comparison with what is given to her and how that small bit is feeble—

full of faults and failures. The soul is naturally reluctant to dwell on the imperfection of her actions. She prefers to forget about her own efforts and place herself at the mercy of God. Since she has no currency with which to reimburse him, she appeals to the compassion he has always shown to those who miss the mark.

Then maybe God will respond as he did to a certain person who was sitting before a crucifix reflecting with dismay that she had never had anything to give to God or to give up for his sake. The crucified one himself consoled her, saying that he was giving her all the pains and trials he had undergone in his Passion so that she could have them as her own to offer to his Father. According to what this woman told me, she was so enriched by this experience and drew so much comfort from it that she cannot forget it. Whenever she feels miserable she thinks about it, and it soothes her and gives her encouragement.

Since I have dealt with many holy people whose lives are all about prayer, I could recount some other incidents like this one, but I'm holding myself back because I don't want you to think that I'm actually talking about myself. What I've already said should be enough to help you to understand how pleased our Beloved is when we come to know ourselves, when we strive to reflect on our poverty and insignificance, recognizing that whatever we have has been given to us.

And so, friends, this realization demands courage and courage is also required for many other things that happen to souls whom the Beloved has brought to this stage. It seems to me that if we were to truly accept our own powerlessness, we would be both truly humble and truly brave. May the Beloved, being who he is, grant us this holy courage.

Let's return now to this sudden rapture which really does seem to catapult the spirit from the body. On the other hand, it is clear that the person is not dead, even if she herself cannot say whether or not she was in her body at certain moments. What she does feel is that she has been in an entirely different zone from the one that the rest of us live in. In that place, she is shown a light so rarefied that if she were to spend the rest of her life here on earth trying to imagine that light and other things revealed to her there, it would be impossible for her to reach them.

In a single instant, the soul is taught so many different things that she could never fit together a thousandth of them, no matter how many years she labored with her mind to create some kind of systematic order. What I'm talking about here still lies in the realm of mental imagery and is not yet a purely transcendental vision. We see things with the eyes of the soul much more clearly than with the body's eyes. There are some things we understand without words. If a person in this state encounters saints, she knows them as well as if she had spent a lot of time with them.

Sometimes the soul will see a host of angels with their master. Sometimes she will see other things not meant to be spoken of. Sometimes the soul will see neither with the eyes of the body nor the eyes of the mind but with a transcendent wisdom that I cannot explain. Maybe someone who has experienced this and has a greater gift with words would know how to express this, but it seems to me that it would be exceedingly difficult. Whether or not the soul is in the body while all this is taking place I couldn't say. I myself wouldn't swear that the soul stays in the body or that the body is robbed of its soul.

I have often thought about how the soul and the spirit are really one thing, like the sun and its rays. The sun remains high in the sky but its beams are so powerful that they effortlessly reach the earth. While the soul stays still, the warmth that shines on her from the true Sun of Justice causes some higher part of her to rise above itself. Oh, I don't know what I'm talking about! Think of a gun. As fast as the bullet shoots out when the trigger is pulled, the spirit takes flight. I'm not sure what else to call it but that: an inner flight. And, although this movement unfolds in silence, it is absolutely unmistakable. While the spirit is far beyond itself—from all that can be understood—great things are revealed. When the spirit returns to itself, the soul finds herself reaping extraordinary benefits. Compared to the things she has seen, worldly things look like garbage.

From then on, life on earth is painful to her. Whatever used to feel good to her seems empty and meaningless now. The Beloved has given her a glimpse of her future. Like the Israelites who brought back tokens from the Promised Land, God gives the soul a sign of the place where she will be able to rest at last, and so inspires her to endure the trials of this arduous path. You may wonder how something that passes so quickly can be so beneficial. Only a person who has had this experience will be able to understand the value of the blessings it leaves inside the soul.

This rapture clearly has no connection to the spirit of evil, nor does it have anything to do with the imagination. Neither of these could possibly reveal things that leave the soul with such serenity, calm, and virtue. Three especially sublime benefits are harvested in the soul by these raptures. The first is knowledge of the greatness of God. The more we see of this greatness, the more deeply conscious we become. The second is humility through self-knowledge. How can something like the soul, so limited by comparison to the Creator of such magnificence, dare to dishonor him? In this state, she can scarcely raise her eyes to him! The third is a loss of appetite for worldly things. Her only interest in the things of the world lies in their capacity to be used in the service of such a great God.

These are the jewels the Spouse is starting to give to his bride. They are so precious that the soul would never risk losing them. These trysts between the soul and her Beloved engrave themselves so deeply in her memory that it is impossible for her to forget them; she lives for the day when she can enjoy him unbroken forever. If she did forget, it would be her own fault. But the Spouse who gives these blessings also has the power to give her the grace not to lose them.

Well, getting back to the soul's need for courage, I ask you: does this really seem to you to be a trivial thing? When the soul loses her senses, she doesn't understand why they have gone away and she feels as if she were separated from her body. This is scary. She needs the One who gives everything else to give her courage, too. You say that the soul is rewarded well for her fear. So do I.

May he who gives so abundantly be forever praised. And may it please His Majesty that we be worthy to serve him. Amen.

.6.

Along with the wondrous favors God bestows on the soul comes this terrible, beautiful torment: she is filled with longing to unendingly drink of the One who gives these blessings.

She yearns to die. The yearning is so intense that all she can do sometimes is weep, begging God to rescue her from exile. Everything she sees in this life wearies her. She finds some relief in solitude, but the torment always comes back. And yet, without this pain, the soul feels as if something vital were missing.

And so, our little butterfly cannot find any lasting rest. In fact, the tenderness of her love makes her soul so light, any occasion that kindles the fire makes the spirit soar. That's why there are so many uncontrollable raptures in this dwelling. She is incapable of resisting them, even in public. The result is often criticism and persecution. She would like to be free from her fears about this, but others won't allow her to be. The worst offenders can be religious officials.

On the one hand, the soul feels a deep sense of inner security when she is alone with God. On the other hand, she is agitated and upset, afraid that the spirit of evil might find a way to deceive her into betraying the One she loves. What other people say about her doesn't bother her so much anymore, except if she is denounced by her own spiritual guide. As if she could prevent these raptures! She does nothing but ask everyone she meets to pray for her and begs His Majesty to lead her along some other path, since, according to all the people around her, the path she is on is very dangerous. And yet she has found this to be such a beautiful road! Everything she reads and hears and knows about God's commandments tells her that this way will lead her home to him.

No matter how hard she tries, she cannot conjure up the desire for anything else but to abandon herself into his loving embrace. This powerlessness in itself upsets her, because it appears as if she were disobeying her spiritual guide. She has come to believe that the only remedy against deception lies in obedience to her teachers and reverence for God. Knowing that she cannot help committing occasional transgressions distresses her terribly; she would rather be crushed to pieces than knowingly miss the mark.

God gives the soul the most intense desire not to dishonor him in any way and to avoid even the most petty imperfection. If for no other reason, this is why the soul wants to flee from people. She envies those who live in the wilderness. On the other hand, she would like to plunge right into the heart of the world in the hopes of getting even one person to praise God more. For a woman, this urge is generally thwarted. Who will listen to her? She is envious of a man's freedom to go around the world openly spreading the word about who this great God of the multitudes is.

Oh, poor little butterfly, bound by so many chains that keep you from flying wherever you want to go! Have mercy on her, my God. Let her do something toward fulfilling her desires for your honor and glory. Pay no attention to how little she deserves your grace or how undeveloped her nature may be. You are all-powerful, Lord. It is you who rolled back the vast sea and the great river Jordan, allowing the children of Israel to pass through.

But do not feel sorry for this little butterfly. Reinforced by your strength, she can endure any trial. In fact, she is determined to suffer everything for you. Extend your mighty arm, Lord, so that this soul does not have to waste her life in unholy ways. Manifest your greatness in this simple, feminine creature, so that all may see that this greatness is not hers but yours and be moved to give you praise. This is all she wants. She would gladly give a thousand lives, if she had them, so that one single soul might praise you a little more through her. She would consider such lives to be well spent. As it is, she doesn't believe that she is worthy of suffering even the most minor trial for your sake, much less die for you.

I'm not sure why I'm saying all this, friends. I don't understand these things, myself. They must be the effects left by those raptures and ecstasies. The desires they spark in the soul do not pass but remain blazing so brightly in the heart that whenever an occasion arises to reveal them, it is clear that they are not the result of some made-up experience but the fruits of an absolutely real one.

Why do I say that these longings remain? Sometimes, in the most insignificant matters, the soul feels like a coward. She can get so frightened and so timid that she doesn't think she has the courage to do anything at all. At this point, the Beloved leaves her to her own nature. That way she sees that any ability she has ever had to take action is bestowed on her by His Majesty. This realization does the soul a lot of good. She sees this truth with such clarity that her small self is annihilated, and she is left with a deeper sense of God's greatness and mercy. He is happy to use the smallest occasion to demonstrate his goodness.

Be mindful of one thing, friends, when it comes to these great desires to see your Beloved: they can be so oppressive that it would be best to avoid feeding them and rather to try to distract yourselves if you can. I'll tell you later about some desires that simply cannot be ignored. But these are desires that you can sometimes let go of. Resign yourselves to God's will. Repeat what Saint Martin said: "Lord, if I am still necessary to your people, I won't refuse to live. Thy will be done." If you are tormented by longing, this practice might be helpful.

Desires like these are generally found in very advanced souls. It's possible for the spirit of evil to stir up false versions of them to fool us into thinking we are advanced, so it is always a good idea to walk with caution. Still, I don't think that the spirit of evil would be able to fill the soul with the deep quietude and serenity this sacred suffering gives her. The feelings that false longing can arouse may be passionate, but they are more like the turmoil we feel about worldly problems. A person who has had no experience of the difference between authentic and unauthentic longing will mistake all her desires as being something great and will stimulate this feeling as much as she can. This could be seriously harmful to her health. True spiritual distress does not just go away. Or, if it does, it comes right back.

You should consider the possibility that this distress is not divine in origin but is caused by a weak constitution. This is especially true of hypersensitive people who cry over every little thing. A thousand times they convince themselves that they are weeping for God, but it isn't true. For a while, every word they hear about God may trigger an abundant flow of tears. It could be that what is happening is that some mood has settled on the heart and that it is this, more than love of God, that is triggering the tears.

It seems like these people will never stop crying. They have heard that tears are good, and so they don't even try to

control them. That's all they want to do: cry. They do everything they can to induce it. The spirit of evil may be trying to
weaken these people so that after they're finished crying they
don't have the energy to pray or engage in spiritual discipline.

I can almost hear you asking: "What am I supposed to
do? You're telling me that everywhere I look there's danger.
Even in something as good as tears you tell me there can be
deception. Maybe you, Mother, are the one being deceived."
Sure, it could be that I am. But believe me, I'm not talking
about something I haven't directly observed in some people.
I don't happen to be tender like that, myself. In fact, my own
hardheartedness worries me sometimes. Although, when the
inner fire is intense, it melts any heart, distilling it like elixir
in a crucible. You will know beyond doubt when the tears
come from this source, because they will be soothing and
comforting rather than agitating and exhausting. If there is
any good in the false tears it is that, as long as there is humility present, they may harm the body but they can't hurt the
soul. In any case, it's wise to be suspicious of the cause for
any tears.

The point is, let's not think that as long as we are crying
we are accomplishing what we need to do. Instead, let's set
our hands to working hard and cultivating virtue. That's all
that matters. Let the tears come when God sends them and
not when we think we're supposed to stir them up. Tears
from God irrigate this dry land and help yield sweet fruit.
The less attention we pay to these true tears, the more it will
rain. This is the water that falls from heaven. The tears we

draw out by actively excavating for them cannot compare to the tears that come from God. When we depend on our own efforts, we tire ourselves out with all that digging. Sometimes we don't even find a puddle of water, let alone a gushing well.

And so, friends, I think it's better to place ourselves in the presence of the Beloved, gazing upon his greatness and his mercy, at the same time that we acknowledge our own simplicity. Leave it to him to give us what he wants, whether it be wetness or dryness. He knows best what we need. Believing in this, we can walk in peace, and the spirit of evil will have less opportunity for playing tricks on us.

In the midst of these divine experiences, which are painful and delicious at the same time, the Beloved sometimes fills the soul with feelings of exultation and a strange kind of prayer that she cannot understand. I'm mentioning it here so that if it happens to you it will make sense and you will joyfully praise him. I think that what's going on here is that the faculties are immersed in profound union while, at the same time, the Beloved leaves both the faculties and the senses free to enjoy this joy without any understanding of what they are enjoying or how they are enjoying it.

Does this sound like sheer drunkenness? But that's how it feels: like inebriation. The joy in the soul is so great that she doesn't want to enjoy it all by herself. Her impulse is to shout it from the rooftops so that everyone can help her praise our Lord. Everything she does is directed toward praising him. Oh, what festivals and exhibitions the soul would put on, if she could, so that the whole world would witness her joy! She feels like she has found herself. Like the father of the prodigal son, she wants to prepare a feast and invite the whole town to celebrate. The soul sees that she is in an unassailable place of safety, at least for the moment. I think she's right about this. There is such serenity and joy in the most intimate place inside the soul that it cannot possibly have come from the spirit of evil. All this happiness stirs the soul to sing God's praises.

To keep silent and attempt to contain this great impulse of joy is no small anguish. How could she hold it back? This must have been what Saint Francis went through when he was wandering through the countryside crying out loud and the robbers attacked him. He told the thieves that he was the messenger of the great King. Other saints must be feeling this when they go into the desert where they can freely proclaim the greatness of God and praise him with all their hearts, like Francis did. I knew a very holy man named Peter of Alcantara. Based on the way he lived, I believe he was a saint. Peter behaved like this, but the people called him crazy.

Oh, what blessed madness, friends! If only God would give it to us all! He has been exceedingly good to us to bring us to this community where, if you experience a divine favor and tell your friends about it, you will not be criticized as you would be in the world but rather encouraged to praise him even more. There are so few people to praise him out there that it's no wonder someone would be looked upon with suspicion if they went around proclaiming his wonders.

Oh, what disastrous times we live in and how wretchedly we must live in them! Souls who get to escape from the misery are fortunate indeed. Such joy wells up in my heart some-times when I see the friends gathered together. We are so blessed to live in this spiritual community where it is our practice as well as our delight to praise God day and night. These praises rise clearly from the depths of the soul. Sing his praises often, friends. When one of you starts singing, it inspires the rest. What better use do we have for these tongues of ours? There are so many excellent reasons to praise him!

May it please His Majesty to give us this prayer often, since it is so righteous and rewarding. It is a supernatural thing, so we cannot attain it on our own. It may last all day. The soul will amble around like someone who has had too much to drink but not so much that it has made him lose his senses completely. Or she will be like someone suffering from a mental imbalance who has not lost all his reason but can't shake off something he's gotten stuck in his imagination and no one else can free him from it either.

These are crude comparisons for something so precious, but I can't come up with any clever ones. The joy in this state of prayer makes a person so forgetful of herself and of all other things that she doesn't notice anything else and can speak of nothing else. All she can do is praise God.

Let's support this soul, my friends. Why should we want to be more sober than that? What could possibly make us happier than to share her intoxication?

And may all creatures come to our assistance forever and ever. Amen, amen, amen!

Those of you, friends, who have not yet attained these uncommon blessings from God might think that the souls who have received these special favors must be so secure that they have nothing to lament—no fears, no imperfections— and can just relax now into enjoying the Beloved forever. Those of you who have experienced these particular states will know what I'm about to say: it would be a mistake to think that these states of prayer bring an end to suffering. On the contrary: the more you receive from God, the more it hurts to see where you have missed the mark. I myself believe that this pain will never go away until we reach the place where nothing can disturb us.

It's true that sometimes this pain hurts more intensely

than at other times. Sometimes it carries one flavor, other times a different one. But the soul is not thinking about the suffering she must undergo to pay for her mistakes. What she is concerned about is that she has been ungrateful to the One to whom she owes so much, who so clearly deserves to be served by her, to be adored. As God reveals his greatness to the soul, her awareness of his plenitude is expanded. She is shocked by how brazen she has been; her lack of respect makes her cry. The foolish mistakes of her past strike her as so flagrant, she cannot stop grieving over them. She can't bear it when she remembers how she turned away from so great a Beloved for such meaningless things. Her own folly is much more prominent in her consciousness than her recollection of the favors she receives, no matter how beautiful these blessings may have been and still are. It's as if a mighty river were running through the soul. Sometimes it brings a wave of sweetness. Sometimes the bitterness of the soul's own imperfections cling to her banks like a bitter slime. It's the bitterness she remembers, and this is a heavy cross to bear.

I know a certain person who used to wish to die so that she could see God. Then she started wishing to die so that she could be free from the unrelenting pain she was feeling about ever having been ungrateful to the One who had been so good to her. She didn't think that anyone else's wickedness could match up to hers. After all, she reasoned, look at how much God has had to put up with from her and for how long! And look how bountifully he has blessed her anyway!

Souls in this state have no fear of the underworld. Occasionally they are afraid that they might offend God, and this disturbs them deeply. But their anxiety is focused on the possibility that God might release them from his hand and that they will turn around and offend him, plunging them into as miserable a condition as they were in before he bestowed his blessing. They don't care one bit about their own pain or glory. Their only reason for not wanting to linger in limbo has nothing to do with a reluctance to suffer; it's that they cannot be with God in that place.

No matter how favored by God a soul may be, I wouldn't consider it safe for her to forget all about the wretched state she used to be in. As upsetting as this can feel, reflecting on it can benefit other souls. It could be that I hold this opinion because I myself have been so wicked that I can't just forget it. Those of you who have been good will not have to carry this pain, although as long as we live in earthly bodies we will make mistakes.

The belief that our Beloved has already forgiven our transgressions and forgotten all about them offers no relief. In fact, it has the opposite effect on the soul at this stage. Reflecting on the infinite goodness of God, who grants such remarkable blessings to someone who has not even come close to earning them, only fuels the fire of her suffering.

It also may occur to you that any soul who has enjoyed exalted states has no use for meditating on specific things like the sacred humanity of Jesus Christ. Isn't this a soul who is already immersed in pure loving? I have written about this subject elsewhere and have been accused of not knowing what I was talking about. These critics suggest that the Beloved leads us along certain paths and that once a soul has passed through the beginning stages of prayer it's better for her to meditate on formless divinity and stay away from earthly images. No matter how eloquently they may contradict me, they cannot get me to admit that this abstract practice is a good thing.

Some souls have convinced themselves that they are incapable of thinking about the Passion, visualizing the Blessed Mother, or reflecting on the qualities of the saints. I cannot imagine what their problem is! Remembering the holy ones who came before us can be very inspiring and encouraging. It isn't possible for those of us in mortal bodies to remain in a perpetual state of transcendence over corporeal things, burning night and day in the fire of pure divine love. That's for angelic spirits, not for human beings. It's important for us to think about, talk to, and cultivate real relationships with those who once lived on this earth and accomplished great things for God. It's even more important to stay connected to Christ, in whom lies all our good and all our help.

Quite a few people have told me that the Beloved brought them into a state of pure contemplation and that they just wanted to stay there forever. This is impossible to do. Still, something of the blessing the Beloved bestows stays inside the soul so that afterwards she can't really engage in discursive meditation about the mysteries of the Passion and the life of Christ, anymore. I don't know why. But this inability to meditate is a very common effect of that depth of contemplation.

I believe that this is because discursive meditation is all about seeking God and that once God has been found the soul doesn't see any reason to wear herself out searching for him through the limited intellect when the will can take her straight to him. Why use the cumbersome faculty of reason when the generous faculty of will is already on fire? There is nothing wrong with setting the intellect aside for a while, but it is impossible to avoid altogether—at least until the soul reaches the final two dwellings. In fact, the soul will lose time trying to bypass the mind. The will often needs the assistance of the intellect to enkindle it.

This is an important point, friends, so pay attention. The soul desires to be wholly engaged in loving and doesn't want to be distracted by anything else. But no matter how badly she might want this exclusive focus, she can't have it that way. Although the will stays alive, the flames that fueled it start to burn out. Someone has to blow on the embers if it's going to radiate heat. Would it be a good idea for a soul suffering from this kind of empty aridity to wait for fire to come down from heaven and burn up the sacrifice she has made of herself to God, like our father Elijah did? No, definitely not.

It's not right for the soul to expect miracles, either. Remember: the Beloved works miracles in the soul when he chooses. I don't think he wants us to go around thinking we're entitled to blessings on demand. He wants us to stay mindful of our limitations and help ourselves in every way we can. I myself believe that this is a healthy attitude to maintain until we die, no matter how sublime our heights of prayer may be.

It is true that anyone the Beloved brings to the seventh dwelling rarely, if ever, needs to practice discursive meditation. If I can remember, I will explain why this is the case when we get to that place. A soul in this state walks with Christ in a wondrous way, communing with both his human nature and his divinity. But when the fire in the will grows cold and the soul no longer feels God's presence, she must actively seek it. This is what the bride does in the Song of Songs and this is what His Majesty wants us to do. Let us ask the creatures who it is that made them, as Saint Augustine did in his *Meditations*, I believe (or was it his *Confessions?*). Why sit around waiting for God to bestow on us what he gave us before? In the early stages of our practice of prayer, God may wait for a year or more to give us this fire. Maybe many years. His Majesty knows why and it's none of our business. We know the path to pleasing God: it lies in the commandments and the counsels. We should follow them diligently, reflecting on the life and death of Christ and on all that he has done for us. Let the rest come when the Beloved wills it.

People in that state might argue that they can't pause to dwell on forms. Maybe they're right, in a way. We already know that it's one thing to reason with the discursive mind and quite another for the memory to convey truths to the discursive mind. You might say that you don't understand what I'm talking about here, and it could be that I don't understand the matter well enough myself to explain it adequately. But I'll do the best I can.

When I talk about discursive meditation, what I mean is extended intellectual reflection: intentional spiritual thought. For example, we may be thinking about the favor God granted us by giving us his only Son. We don't stop there. We go on to consider the mysteries of Christ's whole glorious life. Maybe we begin by musing on his prayer in the Garden and follow it through with our minds all the way to his death on the cross. Or maybe we pick an episode of the Passion, like the arrest, for instance. We meditate on this mystery, exploring all the things there are to think and feel about it, such as the betrayal of Judas and the flight of the apostles. This kind of prayer is admirable and virtuous.

Those whom God has elevated to supernatural states of perfect contemplation claim that they can no longer practice this kind of prayer. They are correct. I just don't know why. But I do not think such a person is right if she says that she never dwells on the mysteries at all, especially if she is present when the Church celebrates these things. It isn't possible for a soul who has received so much from God to forget all about the forms, either. So many precious signs of love! These are the living sparks that ignite the soul more ardently in her love of our Beloved. The soul does not understand these mysteries in any kind of ordinary way; she knows them in a transcendent, perfect way.

The first thing the mind does is to picture some holy

scene and then stamp it into the memory so that the mere sight of our beloved Christ fallen to his knees in the Garden, drenched in that terrible sweat, is enough to occupy the intellect not only for an hour but for many days. We look with a simple gaze at who he is. We acknowledge how unconscious we have been in the face of such suffering. Soon the will responds. Maybe it is not moved with profound suffering but at least with a simple urge to serve, to offer some kind of compensation for such a great favor, and to suffer something for the One who has suffered so much for us. Other desires like this get triggered in the will, corresponding to whatever it is that the mind and memory are dwelling on. The deep tenderness this stirs in the soul might make her think she can go no further in discursive meditation on the Passion. This inability to think makes her think that she will never be able to think again!

If a person is not already doing this meditation practice, she should try it. I promise that it will not be an obstacle to higher prayer. In fact, I think it would be a big mistake to avoid it. If while she is involved in discursive meditation the Beloved decides to suspend the intellect, that is well and good. He will be making her transcend the mind in spite of herself! If this happens, the soul should not consider it to be a problem but a great help toward everything that is good. The problem would arise if she labored hard with her intellect at that point. I do believe that discursive meditation is impossible for souls who have advanced to this state of prayer. Maybe some souls could still practice it in that place: God does lead souls by many paths. But souls who travel the road of the mind should not condemn those who bypass it or judge them as being incapable of appreciating the mysteries encompassed by our good Jesus Christ. On the other hand, no one—no matter how spiritual he may be—is going to get me to believe that intentionally turning away from these mysteries is beneficial, either.

Some beginners on the spiritual path—and even some advanced practitioners—attain the Prayer of Quiet, drink in the sweetness there, and then decide that they should stay in this state permanently. Take my advice: let it go. It is neither good nor even possible to remain perpetually absorbed. Life is long and filled with strife. We need to look to Christ as our role model; see how he handled his trials. Look at his disciples and saints: how did they bear their burdens? Allow them to teach us to bear ours more perfectly. Christ is too good a companion for us to turn away from him and his most Blessed Mother. He is pleased when we grieve over his suffering, even if it means neglecting our own comfort and convenience.

Anyway, friends, consolations in prayer are not such a common occurrence that they eclipse everything else. I would be suspicious of anyone who claimed that her bliss was continuous—I mean, anyone who claims that she is too busy being absorbed all the time to reflect on Christ's Passion. You should be suspicious, too. Strive to free yourselves from such an error and resist absorption with all your might. If your own efforts are not enough, ask for the opportunity to serve, dedicating yourself to a task that requires such care and concentration that this danger will naturally melt away. Continuous absorption can be dangerous for your brain and head.

I think that by now I've conveyed to you that, no matter how spiritual a soul may be, it's not wise to reject all corporeal forms. Meditating on the holiness of humanness is not unholy. Some people try to remind us that Christ told his disciples that it was appropriate for him to leave them. I can't stand this interpretation. I'll bet you anything he didn't say this to his most Blessed Mother! She was solid in her faith. She knew he was both God and man. Although she loved him even more than the disciples did, her love was so perfect that his form was not an obstacle but a vehicle for liberation. The faith the disciples had must have been a little shaky in the beginning; it became stronger, later. And those of us alive now have even greater reason to have firm faith.

I tell you, friends, this is a dangerous path. The spirit of evil will try to lead us away from our devotion to the most blessed mystery of Christ's humanity.

The mistake I used to make wasn't quite this extreme. What I did was that I stopped taking delight in thoughts of Christ and instead waited around for absorption and the consolation it brings. Then I realized clearly that I was on the wrong track. Since it's not possible to sustain a state of absorption, my thoughts went flitting around all over the place. My soul felt like a bird flying around and around, unwilling or unable to alight anywhere, losing a lot of time, not making any progress in virtue or improvement in the practice of prayer. I couldn't understand why I was unable to focus. It seemed to me that what I was doing was correct.

Finally, one day I talked to a person who was a servant of God and explained my method of prayer. He gave me some helpful advice, which clearly demonstrated how mistaken I had been. I couldn't help but regret that there was ever a time when I failed to realize that my great loss—of tangible imagery of Christ and of the path he had to take—could never result in gain. And even if I could get something out of it, I wouldn't want it unless it came through him from whom all real blessings come to us.

May he be praised forever. Amen.

.8.

I have told you, friends, that the further a soul journeys on her path, the more she finds herself accompanied by the good Jesus. When His Majesty wills it, we can't do anything other than walk with him all the time. All you have to do is look around you to see that this is true. Doesn't His Majesty communicate himself to us in wonderful visions and other manifestations? Isn't it obvious that he loves us?

If the Beloved grants you any of the favors I am about to describe (and if he grants me the ability to describe them with any success!), I don't want you to be afraid. Praise him. Praise him even if he doesn't grant you these favors. What we are doing is giving thanks that he who is filled with all majesty and all power is pleased to commune like this with a creature.

It may happen that while the soul is not in any way expecting it she will feel the presence of Christ beside her. She sees him with neither the eyes of the body nor the eyes of the soul. This is called an intellectual vision; I don't know why.

I saw that God had granted this favor to a certain person. She was frightened at first because, since she couldn't see anything, she didn't know what was happening to her. She did know with absolute certainty, however, that it was Christ. Though invisible to the senses, he revealed himself so clearly that she could not doubt it was him. What I mean is, she could not doubt that she was having this vision and that the experience itself was real. What she couldn't be sure about was whether or not the experience was from God. Even though the effects strongly indicated that it was, she still worried. She had never heard of an intellectual vision; she never suspected there was such a thing. But she realized that Christ had been talking with her all along. Until the Beloved granted her this favor, she never knew who it was that had been speaking with her, though she understood the words. It's not a visual revelation, which passes very quickly. It can last for many days, sometimes even more than a year.

This woman I am speaking about went to her spiritual advisor, quite disturbed. He asked her how she knew that it was Christ who was with her, since she didn't actually see anything. He demanded that she describe his face, but she explained that she never saw any face. She said that she had already told him everything she could. All she knew was that he was the one who had been speaking to her all along and that this vision was real. Although other people tried to sow seeds of doubt in her heart, they could not sprout. She was incapable of doubt, especially when Christ said to her, "Be not afraid; it is I."

These words had such power that from then on her confidence in the authenticity of the vision was unshakable. It strengthened her and left her glad for such excellent companionship. She saw clearly how this vision helped her walk with continual remembrance of God. It seemed that the Beloved was always looking at her, and so she avoided doing anything that might displease him. When she had the urge to speak to His Majesty—in prayer or outside it—she sensed that he was so near he couldn't help but hear her. It's not as if she could listen to his words whenever she wanted to, but he spoke to her at unexpected times, when she needed it. She felt him walking at her right side. She didn't experience this with the ordinary senses that tell us there is someone next to us, but in a subtler, more delicate way that transcends explanation. Yet it is absolutely unmistakable.

This vision leaves the soul even more certain than other revelations; the ones that come in the form of sensory imagery can deceive us. Deception is not possible in an intellectual vision. The effects it creates inside the soul are so beneficial that the spirit of evil could never be responsible for them. The experience could not be the result of mental imbalance, either. The soul is washed with profound serenity. All she wants is to please God, and she rejects anything that does not lead her to him.

Later, this woman I've been telling you about attained a clear realization that her vision did not come from the spirit of evil, and this became increasingly apparent as her journey unfolded. Still, I do know that at times this woman felt intensely confused and afraid because she couldn't figure out why such goodness had come to her. The reason I know about this is that she and I were so close, nothing happened in her soul that I didn't know about, and so I'm a reliable witness. Believe me, everything I have said is true.

This radical humility and awe are favors from the Beloved. If the vision came from the spirit of evil, it would have the opposite effects. The soul understands that this is a gift from God and that no human effort could create the experience. The person going through it can in no way mistake it for her own but knows it to be a gift from the hand of God.

In my opinion, some of the other experiences we've talked about are more sublime, but this one bears with it a special knowledge of God. The constancy of divine companionship gives rise to a most tender love for His Majesty. It intensifies the soul's desire to surrender herself completely to serving him. It awakens a more profound purity of consciousness because the presence at her side makes her more sensitive to everything. We already know, of course, that God is present in all that we do, but it is in our nature to lose sight of this fact. In a vision like this, it's impossible to forget, because the Beloved himself awakens the soul to the divine presence beside her. As the soul's love for the one she knows to be walking with her grows more real and more constant, the other favors we've talked about become more common, as well.

On the whole, the value of the vision is proven by the wonderful ways the soul grows as a result of it. The soul is deeply grateful to the Beloved for bestowing such a blessing on someone who hasn't earned it. She wouldn't exchange this gift for any treasure or pleasure on earth. When the Beloved decides to take the vision away, the soul feels terribly lonely. But all the effort she could possibly make would not bring back that sweet companionship. The Beloved gives it when he wills it to be given; it cannot be acquired but only humbly received.

Sometimes, by the way, the vision is of some saint, and this kind of companion can be very helpful to us, too.

If she can't see anything, how can the soul know that this presence is Christ, or his most glorious Mother, or a saint? The soul will not be able to explain it. She herself does not understand how she knows it with such absolute certainty. It's easier to identify Christ when he speaks. But even when it's a saint who appears and doesn't say a word, the soul knows that he has been sent by the Beloved to be her companion and help her. Isn't that marvelous? There are all kinds of spiritual experiences that cannot be explained, but they teach us about the limitations of our nature and highlight the sublime wonders of God. We can't figure these things out. All we can do is receive them with gratitude and awe.

Since the Beloved does not grant these blessings to everyone, the soul should cherish them when they come and strive to do ever greater service, knowing that it is God who enables her to serve. In this way, she realizes that being the recipient of such grace does not make her superior over others. In fact, she sees herself as being more inept than anyone on earth when it comes to serving God and that no one else has a greater obligation to serve him than she does. Any fault that she commits pierces her to the core of her being, and rightly so.

Any of you whom the Beloved leads along this path will recognize the effects I've been describing. These are what will convince you that this vision is not a delusion or a fantasy. Remember: a vision brought on by the spirit of evil could never last so long or leave the soul with such wondrous benefits, clothing her in deep inner peace. Something so bad could never do something so good, even if it wanted to. If the vision came from an evil source, the soul would immediately start putting on some outward show, trying to convince everyone of how much more important and spiritual she is than anybody else. Instead, the soul goes around hopelessly attached to the Beloved, her thoughts totally centered on him. This enrages the spirit of evil, which may lash out and try to deceive her again, but not often. Besides, God is so faithful that he will protect a soul whose only goal is to please His Majesty and devote her entire life to his honor and glory.

He will not let evil penetrate her nor will he allow her to be deceived.

My point is and will continue to be this: these favors from God inspire the soul to walk with beauty and grace, which inspires him to give her even more. If he sometimes allows the spirit of evil to challenge the soul, he will make sure that the evil one is defeated. And so, friends, if any of you travels this road, do not be afraid. At the same time, it's a good thing to stay alert and step with care, because if you become overconfident you could stumble and fall. Check to see if the effects of the vision harmonize with what I've told you about. If not, that's a sign that the vision probably does not come from God.

In the beginning, it's better to share this experience only with someone you trust to keep it confidential. It should be an intelligent person who has studied broadly, because people of learning can shed light on these things. It's best to speak with a deeply spiritual person, but if there is no such person around, then seek out the educated one. A person who is both educated and spiritual, of course, would be ideal. If they tell you the vision is a fantasy, don't worry. A fantasy may not help much, but it can't harm you, either. Throw yourself at the mercy of the divine Majesty, asking that he not let you be deceived. If they tell you that your vision comes from the spirit of evil, you have something to worry about. But anyone with any real spiritual sensitivity will know from the effects the vision has produced in you when this is not the case. If he says such a thing anyway, I know that the Friend who walks with you will console and reassure you and that he will illumine the heart of your confidant so that he in turn may illumine you.

Maybe the person advising you has a cultivated spiritual practice of his own. So what? If he has not yet been led by the Beloved along this path, then what you tell him will scare him and he will judge you hastily. That's why I'm recommending that you choose someone who is both knowledgable and wise. Even though it may seem like all is well with you, people who care about you should encourage you to seek this counsel if you feel you need it—for your sake and theirs.

Once you have consulted with the appropriate person, be still and don't keep talking about it. Sometimes, even when the soul has nothing to fear, the spirit of evil stirs such doubts in her that she cannot be satisfied with a single consultation. At other times, if her advisor hasn't had much experience, a soul like this may scare him and he will belabor the point and even turn something that should have been kept a secret into a public spectacle.

When this happens, it opens the soul to persecution and torment. There she was, thinking she had confided in only one person, and it turns out the whole world knows about her private vision. Judging from the way things are going these days, I could anticipate that a drama like this could attract many problems, not only to her as an individual but to her spiritual community as a whole. I recommend a high degree of discretion, both to the soul who has had this vision and to her spiritual guide.

Also, remember that just because someone you may be advising has had a spiritual experience of this kind, it doesn't make her any more special than anyone else. The Beloved sees what each of us needs and guides us accordingly. Assuming we can cooperate, the purpose of this journey is to make us better servants of God. Sometimes it's the weakest among us whom God leads along this path, so we have no reason to either approve or condemn them. Our only valid criteria for judgment are the virtues in the soul who is serving God. Is she humble, detached from personal desires, and is her conscience pure? If so, she is holy. Yet, here on earth, there is very little we can know with certainty. We have to wait until the true judge gives each of us what we deserve. In heaven, we will be surprised to discover how different his judgment is from what we thought it would be in this life.

May he be forever praised. Amen.

. 9 .

It's time to explore the experience of visual revelations—sometimes referred to as imaginative visions, because they take the form of images. People say that this is an experience in which the spirit of evil has more opportunity to interfere than in other kinds of spiritual experiences. Maybe so. But when these visions do come from the Beloved, they seem to be more helpful and more useful than other kinds, because they match up more with our nature as creatures. Of course, the visions that the Beloved reveals to us in the final dwelling surpass all others! There's no question of this.

Please reflect back for a moment on what I told you about how Christ reveals himself to the soul in an intellectual vision. It's as if we held a gold box containing a precious stone of high value and healing powers. Even though we have never actually seen the jewel, we know that it's there. We don't need to see it to believe that it's valuable, as long as we carry it with us and feel its potency. We have experienced its power to cure us of certain maladies that no other medicine could touch.

Still, we don't dare to open the box and look at the stone. Nor could we even if we tried. The only one who knows how to open this container is the owner of the jewel. He has loaned it to us for our good. The box belongs to him, and so he keeps the key with him. When he wants us to see what's inside, he will open it. He will also take the jewel back whenever he feels like it. And sometimes he does.

Let's say that one day the owner of the miraculous stone decides to open the box, for the benefit of the person borrowing it. Once she has seen the beautiful brilliance of the jewel, it will remain engraved in her memory forever, so that she can easily recall its special splendor. This makes her very happy.

That's what happens when an intellectual vision is supplemented by a visual revelation. When the Beloved is pleased to bring greater consolation to the soul, he might reveal to her an aspect of his most sacred humanity. He does this in whatever way he thinks is best for the soul: sometimes in the form of Jesus as he was when he walked the earth; sometimes as the resurrected Christ. The vision happens so quickly it can be compared to a streak of lightning. Yet this glorious image is burned so deeply into the imagination that I think it will not disappear until the soul encounters it again in a place where she can enjoy it without end.

I'm calling this an "image," but please understand that the person it appears to is not seeing it externally, in the same way that you would view a painting, but internally and fully formed, like something that is really alive. It may even speak to the soul, revealing great secrets. While the soul finds this vision utterly captivating, she can no more easily fix her inner gaze on it than she could stare into the face of the sun with her outer eye, and so it passes swiftly.

I wouldn't know what to say about visions that come through the external sense of sight. You can never be sure about what you haven't experienced, and the person I mentioned, whom I know intimately, has only had the interior variety of vision. The brilliance of this inner revelation is like infused light, like the sun passing through something transparent, like a cloth woven from fibers of diamond. Whenever God grants this blessing, it sends the soul into rapture. What creature could endure such a magnificent sight? Even if a person were to live a thousand years, she could never fit her imagination around the sheer beauty and sweetness of the Beloved's presence. The majesty is so vast that it surpasses the mind's capacity altogether. The soul is overcome by awe.

It's unnecessary to ask the soul how she knows, without being told, who this Beloved is. He reveals himself clearly as the Lord of heaven and earth. An earthly king could never get away with this; he would have to be announced by his retinue, or we wouldn't take him seriously.

Oh, Beloved, how little we lovers know you! You come here in such a tender way to speak with your bride, and she is terror-stricken to look at you. What's going to happen on that day of reckoning when you say in a booming voice, "Depart, you who have dishonored my Father!"?

It's helpful to bear this final judgment in mind. Even Saint Jerome, who was a holy person, stayed focused on this thought. It keeps us conscious, hones our integrity, and gives us perspective on the larger truth of things. If we hold this awareness, then any time we have spent suffering as a result of arduous spiritual discipline will seem like a moment in comparison with eternity. I must tell you that, as imperfect as I have been, I have never been afraid of the torments of the underworld. These pale in comparison with the thought of the anger and disappointment in the Beloved's eyes—those beautiful, kind, gentle eyes—when he stands in the end before the ones who have forsaken him.

I don't think my heart could endure such a sight. I've felt this way my whole life. Imagine how much more a person will have to fear if she has experienced God in a vision. The Beloved has already blessed such a soul in this life by revealing his presence so powerfully to her consciousness that it sends her into unconsciousness! She has tasted his omnipotence, and it has transported her beyond herself. The reason that the soul lingers in that state where her senses are suspended must be that the Beloved is helping her in her weakness by uniting her with his greatness in the sublime communion she is having with him.

If the soul believes that she is actually gazing for a sustained period of time on the face of the Lord, I don't think what she is experiencing is a real vision. Rather, it's some kind of intense mental reflection, forming a certain picture in the imagination. Compared with a true visual revelation, this image is a dead thing.

Quite a few people have told me about becoming so absorbed in their own imaginations that they can actually visualize everything they think about. I don't know if this is caused by poor imaginations or overly efficient intellects. But if they were to receive a true vision, they would immediately see their error and there would be no doubt about what was real. The method these people subscribe to is to compose an image in their own imaginations—to build it in their minds little by little until they have a picture—but the result leaves them cold; it has no enduring effect. Even seeing an external sacred object has more impact on the soul than these fabrications of her own imagination. We shouldn't pay too much attention to these subjective images. We will forget them even more quickly than we forget a dream.

A true vision is not fleeting. And it's not volitional. The last thing a soul is thinking of at the time is that she is about to see something holy. Suddenly, a vision reveals itself whole, throwing the senses and faculties into frightening chaos, only to set them down afterwards in happy peace.

It's like when Saint Paul was thrown to the ground and a storm exploded in the sky. That's what happens in the inner world. There is a powerful stirring, and then all of a sudden everything grows quiet. Such great truths are taught to the soul in this way that she needs no other master. Without any effort on the soul's part, true wisdom overcomes unconsciousness and certainty replaces doubt. This is a gift from God. It endures for some time.

No matter what anyone else may say to try to alarm her, the soul knows that she has not been deceived with this vision. Later, if a person in a position of spiritual leadership plants fear in her heart, God may allow the soul to vacillate a little. She might question whether or not she is deluding herself and wonder why God would grant such blessed favors to someone as insignificant as she is. But the soul doesn't really believe this. The spirit of evil can stir up doubts, just as it can make trouble in those other areas, and these can momentarily compromise the soul's faith. Yet the more challenged a soul is about her spiritual certainty, the more certain she grows. She knows that the spirit of evil could never leave such bountiful blessings inside of her! This is true. The spirit of evil has no power in this deep inner place. The spirit of evil is capable of conjuring up a vision, but it will never carry this same truth and majesty, or leave these transformational results in the soul.

If the person to whom God grants this favor cannot even describe it, how can her spiritual advisor be expected to understand it? If he has not seen the vision himself, it's likely to frighten him. And rightly so! The best thing is to proceed with caution and wait for the fruits of these apparitions to ripen in the soul. Little by little, humility grows deeper; little by little, virtues grow stronger.

If the vision comes from the spirit of evil, it will soon become obvious: a web of untruth clinging to the soul will be a clear sign. If the spiritual advisor has experience and has himself been graced with visions, he will not require much time to be able to distinguish between a vision from God, a trick played by the spirit of evil, and a mental delusion. If God has given him the gift of discernment, he will know what's going on as soon as it's described to him. If he is educated as well as discriminating, it will not matter so much if he has not had the experience himself—he will recognize it perfectly well as being an authentic revelation.

The important thing, friends, is to confide openly in your spiritual advisor. Tell him the truth. I don't mean that you should focus on your mistakes; I mean that you should give a full account of your spiritual practice. If you are unable to do this, then I can't help question whether you are on the right track and if the teachings you are receiving are divine or not. God seems to appreciate honesty and candor. He seems to want us to speak as clearly to his representatives as we would to him. And he seems to be happy when we disclose all our thoughts to our spiritual guide and report on all our spiritual activities, no matter how trivial.

If you are forthcoming about your inner life, you do not have to be anxious or worried. If you are humble and have a calm conscience, even a vision that does not come from God will do you no harm. His Majesty is able to draw goodness out of wickedness. Then the road by which the spirit of evil tried to lead you astray will instead yield greater blessings. You will be so grateful to God for granting you such wonderful favors that you will strive to please him more and more. You will keep his image burning in your heart.

There is much benefit the soul can draw from these opportunities for remembrance the Beloved manifests for her. When she thinks of Christ—of his life and of his Passion—she recalls his most gentle and beautiful face, and she finds this deeply consoling. It's like here on earth: it makes us happier to see someone we know and love who has helped us on our way than to encounter someone we have never met or even heard of. I assure you, remembering God brings comfort and joy.

This kind of vision brings many other blessings, but that's enough for now. I've said a lot already and will say more later. I don't want to tire myself out or bore you by going on. The last thing I want to talk about is this: if you hear that God has granted this favor to other souls, do not beseech him to lead you the same way. It may seem to you to be a very good path—a path to be desired and admired—but there are a few reasons why it would not be wise to ask for it.

First, it shows a lack of humility to demand what you have not earned. A simple laborer would not aspire to be king, because such a thing would seem impossible and he would not feel worthy. A humble soul would have the same feeling about exalted spiritual experiences. I believe that these visions will never be granted to those who crave them. God first gives the soul depth of self-knowledge. How else is a soul with such lofty ambitions going to realize that the Beloved is already doing her a great favor by not banishing her into exile for all the mistakes she has made?

Second, a soul in desire is in greater danger of being deceived. All the spirit of evil needs is to see a door a little bit ajar to squeeze in and play a thousand tricks on us.

Third, when there is great desire, the imagination itself makes a person think that she sees and hears what she is longing for. It's like when you want something intensely and think about it throughout the day and then end up dreaming about it at night.

Fourth, wouldn't it be rather presumptuous of me to try to choose my own path? What do I know? I don't have the divine perspective to see what's best for me. I should leave the arrangements to the Beloved, who knows me and who will lead me along a path that is right for me. May his will be done in all things!

Fifth, do you think the trials suffered by the souls to whom God does grant these visions are light ones? No. They are massive and they are manifold. How do you know if you would even be able to bear them?

Sixth, you may discover that the very thing you hoped would bring you bounty brings only privation, like when Saul lost everything by becoming king.

There are even more reasons than these, friends. Believe me, the safest thing is to want only what God wants. He knows us better than we know ourselves and he loves us. Let's place ourselves in his hands so that his will may be done in us. If we consciously maintain this intention, we cannot go wrong. Besides, it's not as if the more visions you receive the greater glory you get. On the contrary: souls who receive these favors have a greater obligation to serve.

There are many holy people who have never received one of these favors. There are people who receive them but are not holy. Don't think that these visions are continuous, either. Rather, each time the Beloved grants them, they are accompanied by arduous trials. And so, the soul does not think about how she's going to get more of them but only how to make the best use of what she has already received.

It is true that these visions must help elevate a soul toward more perfect virtue, but a soul who has attained virtue through her own hard work will benefit much more. I'm thinking of a couple of people to whom the Beloved granted such favors. One of them is a man. They wanted to serve His Majesty without the consolation of such spiritual delights. They were so eager to suffer that they complained to our Beloved about how he was burdening them with sweet favors; they would have declined the blessings if they could have. Actually, I'm not referring to visions here, because the soul well knows how beneficial these are and how highly they should be regarded. What I'm talking about is the kind of consolation the Beloved offers in contemplation.

In my opinion, these desires are supernatural. They arise in a soul on fire with love. Such souls want the Lord to see that they aren't serving him for pay. They never try to motivate themselves to serve God with the thought that they will be compensated with glory for anything they do. Their only desire is to satisfy their thirsty love. It is love's nature to express itself through service in a thousand ways. If it could, love would find a way to consume the soul entirely within itself. And if it were necessary for her to be annihilated for the greater glory of God, the soul would happily surrender, over and over again.

May he who reveals his greatness by lowering himself to commune with mere creatures be forever praised. Amen.

. IO .

The Beloved communicates himself to the soul through many different kinds of spiritual manifestations. Some come when the soul is deeply troubled, others when the soul is about to undergo a severe trial, and sometimes just for the sheer delight it gives to both the soul and God when he makes this kind of appearance.

There is no need to go into further detail about each variety of vision. The important thing, friends, is that you have a general sense of the nature of each kind and the effects they leave in the soul. This way you won't be harboring the illusion that everything you imagine qualifies as a vision. Also, when you do have a real vision, you will understand that such things do happen, and it won't confuse or upset you. The spirit of evil thrives on disquiet, because inner turmoil distracts the soul from getting lost in loving and praising God.

There are other ways His Majesty communicates himself to the soul that are more sublime and less dangerous. The spirit of evil is, I believe, incapable of counterfeiting them. These experiences are very intimate and difficult to explain. Visual apparitions are easier to describe.

Sometimes, when the soul is in prayer, the Beloved will suddenly suspend her senses and reveal deep secrets to her. These are not visions of his sacred humanity. The soul is seeing into God himself. I use the term "seeing," but it is not a visual revelation; it is a transcendental vision. What is revealed to the soul is that all things can be seen in God because God has all things inside himself. Even though this vision passes in a moment, it engraves itself deeply in the memory and causes the most blessed confusion in the soul. This is a great favor. The soul becomes keenly aware of imperfect acts she has committed while inside of God. If only she had realized that she was dwelling inside the Beloved himself when she was doing those unconscious things!

I'm going to try to draw an analogy to explain this to you. Although what I am saying about living in God is true and it's not the first time we've heard it, we either don't pay any attention to it or we simply don't want to understand it. If we really understood that we are living inside our Beloved, I don't think we could possibly be so presumptuous about many things.

Let's visualize God for a moment as being like a vast and exquisite dwelling. Let's call it a palace. This palace is God himself. Now, can a wicked person get away from this place to commit wicked deeds? No, of course not! The nasty acts take place within the palace itself, that is, within God himself. Oh, terrifying thought! But a thought worthy of reflection. It would be very helpful for those of us who are ignorant of these truths to understand them. If we truly realized that our negative behaviors defile God's sacred space, we could not possibly act with such audacity.

Let's consider the great mercy and compassion of God, friends, who does not summarily destroy us when we miss the mark. Let's remember to be grateful to him. And let's stop feeling so self-righteous whenever anyone does or says anything against us. It is the most appalling thing in the world that God our Creator has to put up with so many bad things committed by his creatures inside of him and then here we are complaining about a word said about us when we weren't there to defend ourselves, which may not have even carried a shred of negative intention in the first place.

Oh, human misery! When, friends, will we ever begin to emulate this great God of ours? Let's not deceive ourselves into thinking that it is some major accomplishment when we suffer a little persecution. Instead, let's eagerly endure everything that comes to us. Let's love the ones who offend us. Has our great God ever stopped loving us? Not for one second! And we have certainly offended him plenty of times. He has very good reason for wanting us all to forgive anyone who has hurt us.

I tell you, friends, that even though this vision of being inside God passes quickly, it is a great favor from the Beloved. If we hold it in our awareness, it will profoundly benefit us.

It may also happen that God very suddenly reveals a truth within himself that utterly transcends explanation, and any truth found in any creature looks like an impenetrable cloud. In this moment of perfect clarity, the soul understands that God alone is truth and can manifest no falsehood. Remember the psalm where David says that every man is a liar? This is what he meant. No matter how many times we hear that verse we will not understand it until we have this revelation. God is pure truth. I'm thinking about that story of Pilate who questioned Christ incessantly and finally, during his Passion, asked him, "What is truth?" And then I reflect on how little we are capable of understanding this ultimate truth here on earth.

I wish I could say more about this, but it's ineffable. What we need to take from this lesson, friends, is a renewed commitment to learn to walk in truth. In this way, we will align ourselves a little more with our God and Spouse. I'm not just talking about not telling lies. As far as I can tell, those of us who live in spiritual community never do lie. What I'm saying is that we should stand up in our truth, before God and all people, in every way we can. We should relinquish any desire for others to regard us as being better than we actually are. In everything we do, we should attribute to God what is his and take responsibility for what is ours. Above all, we should strive to seek truth always. If we do this, we will see the world for what it is: illusion. We will see that it is imper-manent, and we will not be so attached to it anymore.

I was once pondering why it is that our Beloved is so fond of the virtue of humility. Without it ever having occurred to me before, this thought suddenly came to me: It's because God is supreme truth. To be humble is to walk in truth. It is true to say that we ourselves are nothing. Whoever does not understand this walks a lie. Whoever does under-stand this is more pleasing to supreme truth, because she is walking in truth.

May God grant us the favor, friends, of never straying again from this knowing of ourselves. Amen.

Our Beloved grants these blessings to the soul because he desires to treat her as his true bride. Knowing she adores him, he wants to reveal something of his greatness to her. Knowing that she is determined to align herself with his will, he wants to guide her in seeing how to carry out his will in all things.

That's enough for now. I have mentioned these two visions because they seem to me to be the most beneficial. I want you to see that there is no reason to be afraid of these blessings. Instead, we should praise the Lord who gives them to us. In my opinion, neither the spirit of evil nor our own imagination has any power at this level, and so the soul tastes a profound and abiding sweetness here.

.II.

Don't think I've forgotten our little white butterfly. Have all the favors the Beloved has been granting her been enough to satisfy her? you may ask. Can she come to rest now in the place where she will die?

No, definitely not. In fact, she feels worse than ever. Even though she may have been receiving blessings for many years, she goes around sorrowing and sighing because these tastes of her Beloved leave her even more bereft. The more she comes to know the greatness of God, the farther away from him she sees herself as being. Her desire for him mounts. And her love for him increases in proportion to how much she sees the Beloved deserves to be loved.

This longing gradually increases over the years until it

reaches a point of anguish. That's what I want to talk about next. I'm saying "years" here, because I am referring to the experience of that particular person I mentioned earlier. But we cannot, of course, put limits on God. He can elevate the soul to the highest state in a single moment. His Majesty has the power to do whatever he wants, and he wants to do so many things for us! And so the soul is plagued by yearning, by tears and moaning, by all the painful impulses I have mentioned. These symptoms rise from deep wells of love, but they are nothing compared to the experience I am about to describe. It's like a smoking fire—uncomfortable, but we can bear it.

While the soul is walking around in this condition, burning up inside herself, a sudden fleeting thought or some word spoken about how death is still far away deals her a kind of blow. Or she may feel like she is being pierced by a flaming arrow. I don't mean an actual, material arrow. The soul doesn't really know what it is or where it comes from. But whatever it may be, she clearly realizes that it is not an artifact of her own nature. I do not mean that the blow is a physical one, either, but it does inflict a penetrating wound. We don't feel this wound with our earthly skin, in my opinion, but rather in the intimate depths of the soul. It flashes through us like lightning, reducing everything in our worldly nature to dust. During the brief moment this lasts, we cannot remember a thing about our own existence. The experience binds up the faculties in an instant so they are free to do nothing except that which intensifies the pain.

I hope this doesn't sound like an exaggeration. If anything, what I say falls short of the truth, because the experience is indescribable. It is an enfolding of the senses and the faculties, a transporting of the soul beyond anything that doesn't contribute to this profound spiritual distress. The mind is enlivened by the quest to understand why it is that the soul feels estranged from God. His Majesty adds to the intensity by endowing the soul with such vivid knowledge of himself that the pain becomes overwhelming and she cries out loud. She can't help it. And this is a person who is used to suffering! But this pain is different. It cannot be located in the body. It throbs in the innermost part of the soul.

It was from this experience that the person I've been referring to came to understand how much more deeply the soul suffers than the body. This must be like the torment of purgatory, she thought. These souls don't have bodies and look how they suffer: more than the suffering of all those on earth put together. I watched a certain person going through this. She actually thought she was dying. And she was not far off. Although the experience only lasts for a short time, it leaves the body with the feeling of having been torn asunder. The heartbeat during those moments grows so weak that it truly does seem as if the soul were on the brink of permanently giving herself up to God. This is not an exaggeration. As the fire in the soul intensifies, the natural heat of the body cools. A little longer in that state and the soul would have achieved her desire to leave this world behind.

Although this is not, as I have said, a physical kind of

pain, it makes the limbs feel disjointed and, for a few days after the experience, the person who went through it aches all over and doesn't even have the strength to write. In fact, the body never quite recovers from such an experience. The reason the person in this state feels no physical pain while she's in the middle of it must be because what's going on inside of her eclipses her awareness of the body. Think of getting injured: the pain of the injury overrides all other bodily discomforts, even if they're multiple. I myself am living proof of this phenomenon. In the face of that kind of spiritual pain, I don't think the body could feel a thing, even if it were being cut up into little pieces.

Isn't this feeling in itself an imperfection? you will ask. If the soul at this stage is so surrendered to God, why can't she just resign herself to his will? Up till now, this has not been a problem. The soul has spent a lifetime conforming to the will of God. But the faculty of reason is in no condition to take charge of anything at this point. The soul can think of nothing but the object of her grieving, of how cut off she seems to be from the source of all her good. Why bother to keep on living?

The soul feels her solitude to the core of her being. There is not a creature on all the earth who can be her companion. No heavenly being, either. None of these is the One she loves. In fact, all creaturely company is a torment to her. The soul pictures herself as hanging in midair. She can neither find her footing on the earth nor can she ascend to heaven. Her thirst is a fire, but she cannot reach the water. It's not the kind of thirst that can be quenched, anyway. She doesn't even want it to be quenched, except by that water that Christ told the Samaritan woman about. Who is offering this kind of water to the thirsty soul? No one.

Oh, God help me! Beloved, how you torment your lovers! But all this is insignificant compared to what you will give us later. It makes sense that valuable things should cost a lot. Just as those who will enter heaven must be cleansed in purgatory, the soul who will enter the seventh dwelling must be purified by suffering. If she reaches her goal, this pain is a drop that dissolves in boundless bliss, anyway.

This torment surpasses all earthly afflictions, even though it does, in fact, have some secondary physical manifestations in addition to the obvious spiritual suffering. Still, the soul sees her pain as precious—so precious that she can't believe she is worthy to receive it. This insight does not alleviate the suffering one iota. But knowledge of the incomparable value of her pain makes the soul willing to endure it for the rest of her life, if it be God's will. This, of course, would mean dying not only once but over and over again, since the suffering is just like death.

And now, friends, let's consider the plight of souls in the underworld. They are certainly not resigned to the will of God. They have access to none of the consolation or delight God gives to the soul on her journey home to him. They do not view their suffering as beneficial, but they can't stop suffering. Soul-torment, as we've learned, is far more intense than body-torment. The agony of those in the underworld is greater still, because it never lets up. What will become of these poor souls? What pain can we take on in this short life-time that could possibly inoculate us against that horrendous and interminable anguish?

I tell you, it is impossible to describe how vividly the soul feels this interior spiritual pain and how radically it differs from exterior physical pain. You have to experience it to understand. The Beloved himself wants us to understand this. Only then will our true gratitude be awakened and we will give thanks to God for bringing us to a place where, by his sweet mercy, he may set us free and forgive all our mistakes.

Now, where were we? Oh yes, we left the soul in terrible pain. Luckily, the intensity doesn't last too long. Our natural weakness could not endure it for much more than three or four hours, except by some miracle. Once, it only lasted for a quarter of an hour, but it so badly shredded that particular soul that she lost consciousness completely. The whole ordeal was triggered simply by hearing two words: "life unending." This event occurred right in the middle of a conversation the person was having during Holy Week. Throughout this period she had been suffering from such a bout of aridity she hardly knew it was the season of the resurrection.

A soul has no more power to resist rapture than she would have to stop flames from burning her if she was thrown into a fire. She cannot conceal her feelings from oth-ers in this state. Even though witnesses cannot see what is unfolding deep inside her, it becomes clear that she is in danger. It's true that other people can give her a little company, but they seem like shadows to her. All earthly things appear like shadows to an enraptured soul.

If any of you ever has this experience, I want you to know right now that it can be a hazard to your health. In this state, the soul is dying with the desire to die. The intensity of her longing nearly does squeeze the life from her body. This is a terrifying feeling, and she finds herself torn between wishing the pain would let up and wanting to leave her body forever. At the same time, she is aware that fear arises from natural weakness. This offers her a little bit of helpful perspective. There is no real remedy for the suffering until the Beloved himself takes it away. He usually alleviates the pain through a deep rapture or some kind of vision where the true Comforter consoles the soul and gives her strength, renewing her desire to live as long as it is his will for her to be alive.

Such an experience is excruciating, but it impacts the soul in wonderful ways. She loses her fear of any additional trials she might encounter along the way. Compared to the anguish she has been through, other challenges seem like nothing. The benefits of this experience are so numerous that the soul would gladly suffer it all over again. But just as there is no way to resist the rapture when it comes, the soul cannot summon it when she wants it. She must wait patiently until the Beloved wills her to be carried away again in sweet agony.

A quiet contempt for the world has begun to grow in the soul. She discovered that nothing on this earth could help her during her great torment. Now that she sees that only the

Creator can comfort her, she becomes increasingly detached from all creatures. She feels a sharper anxiety about offending him because she has learned that he can torment as well as console.

There are two experiences on the spiritual path that can put a soul in danger of death: one is this unbearable pain and the other is overwhelming joy. Spiritual delight can reach such sublime heights that the soul swoons on the brink of leaving the body. Which, of course, would make her all too happy!

Now you will see, friends, whether or not I was right in saying that great courage is required to walk this path. If you ask the Beloved for these blessings, don't be surprised if he finds a way to answer you like he answered the sons of Zebedee: "Are you able to drink from this chalice?"

I believe that all of us, friends, will respond with a resounding "Yes!" And rightly so. His Majesty gives strength to those of us he sees have need of it. He defends these souls in every way. If they are persecuted or criticized, he stands up for them, as Christ answered for the Magdalene. He may not speak with words but through action.

And at last—oh, at last!—before they die, he compensates them for everything all at once, as you are about to see.

May he be blessed forever and may all creatures praise him. Amen.

Seventh Dwelling

It would be a mistake for you to think that because we have already talked so much about this spiritual path that no more could possibly be said. Since the greatness of God is limitless, his works, too, are without limit. Who could ever run out of things to say about his mercies and wonders? No one! So don't be surprised by all that has been covered and is still left to explore because it is a mere fraction of what there is to tell about him.

God grants us great mercy whenever he communicates these things to any soul in such a way that through her we come to understand them. The more we understand about his communion with creatures, the more we will praise his greatness. We should cultivate reverence for souls in whom our Beloved seems to take such delight. Each of us has a soul, but we forget to value it. We don't remember that we are creatures made in the image of God. We don't understand the great secrets hidden inside of us.

If it be His Majesty's will, may it serve him to move my pen and help me to understand how I might impart to you a taste of the many blessings God reveals to souls he brings home to this final dwelling. With all my heart, I beseech His Majesty to guide me in this. He knows that my sole intention is to uncover his hidden mercies so that his name will be even more passionately praised, more ardently glorified.

For your sake, friends, if not for mine, I hope he grants me this favor. Then you will see how important it is for you to do nothing to thwart the celebration of the spiritual marriage between the Beloved and your soul. This is a coupling that will give birth to countless blessings. You'll see.

Oh, great God! I should be trembling to be taking on something so far beyond what I am worthy to understand. Indeed, I have been in a state of profound confusion, wondering if it would be best for me to simply offer a brief account of this dwelling and be silent. I'm worried that other people might mistake me for someone who knows these things through experience. This thought fills me with shame. I know what I am. And I know what I am not.

On the other hand, I can see how this reluctance could be a kind of weakness. To neglect explaining what I do know about this place would be to fall into temptation. I must not concern myself with your judgments. Let the whole world cry out against me if it means God may be further understood and praised! Besides, I may well be dead by the time anyone reads what I've written here. Blessed is he who lives forever. Amen.

Because of what we suffer and have suffered through our desire for him, our Beloved has already taken us as his spiritual bride. Now, with tender compassion, he brings us into his own dwelling, the seventh, in preparation for the consummation of the spiritual marriage. Just as His Majesty has a room of his own in heaven, so he has a special place inside the soul where he alone dwells. Let's call it another heaven.

It's very important for us, friends, not to think of the soul as dark. Since we cannot see the soul, it appears to be obscure. We are conditioned to perceive only external light. We forget that there is such a thing as inner light, illuminating our soul, and we mistake that radiance for darkness. I have to admit that a soul who is not in grace is, in fact, in darkness. But that is no fault of the Sun of Justice who dwells within everyone and gives us being. It is because souls in that unfortunate condition are incapable of receiving light, as I mentioned in the first dwelling. A certain person came to understand that these unhappy souls are trapped in a kind of dark prison, with their hands and feet shackled. They are blind and deaf. It is impossible for them to do anything good to earn any merit. We should have compassion for these souls, recognizing that there was a time when we were just like them, and trusting that the Beloved can take mercy on them, too.

Let's take special care, friends, and not neglect to pray to him on their behalf. This is the most generous gift we can offer to souls who are lost in grave error. Suppose we came across a lover of God, bound to a post with his hands chained behind him. He's starving to death. It's not that there's a lack of food available. In fact, he's surrounded by delicious things to eat, only he cannot take hold of them and put them in his mouth, even though he is so sick with hunger that it's obvious he's about to draw his last breath and die. This is not just a death of the body but an eternal death. It would be terribly cruel to stand there looking at him and not help him! Well, then, what if your prayers could loosen his chains? You see what I mean. For the love of God, I ask you to always remember such lost souls in your prayers.

But these are not the souls we're talking about, here. We're talking about those who, by the mercy of God, have already atoned for missing the mark and have entered a state of grace. We are not referring to some dark corner where everything is restricted but to a vast inner space with room for a multitude of beautiful dwellings, as you have seen. Isn't it right that the soul should be such a lovely thing, since the Beloved himself has his chamber inside her?

Now, when the time comes for His Majesty to gift the soul with the divine marriage, he leads her into his own dwelling. He wants it to be different this time. It's not that the soul wasn't really united to him before when he gave her raptures or when she entered into the Prayer of Union. In those states, although she was elevated to the highest part of herself, she didn't feel called to enter the very center of her-self as she does now. These distinctions are irrelevant, really. Whether it happens like this or like that, the Beloved joins the soul to himself.

But in the process God strikes the soul blind and deaf, as Saint Paul was struck in his conversion. It renders her inca-pable of perceiving the nature and the flavor of the blessing she's receiving. This only increases her delight when she dis-covers she is next to God. Yet when he unites himself with her at last, she understands nothing. She loses her senses and her reason entirely.

In the seventh dwelling, everything is new. Now our great God is ready to remove the scales from the eyes of the soul so that she can see and understand something of the blessing he is granting her. He does this in a strange and inex-plicable way. The soul enters the innermost chamber through a transcendental vision of the three divine Persons, which imparts to her a particular representation of truth. At first, an incredible clarity descends on the soul like a luminous cloud, setting her spirit on fire and illuminating each of the three aspects of God individually. At the same time, through a wondrous kind of knowledge, she apprehends the truth that all three divine Persons are one substance and one power and one knowing and one God alone.

The soul realizes then that what the rest of us know by faith, you might say, she understands by sight. But this is not a seeing with the eyes of the body or even the eyes of the soul. It isn't a visual revelation. Here, all three Persons communicate themselves to the soul. They speak to her, explaining things, like what Christ meant in the gospels when he said that he and the Father and the Holy Spirit come to dwell inside the soul who loves God and honors his ways.

Oh, Lord help me! There's a big difference between believing these words by hearing them and being led to understand the truth they represent in this direct and wondrous way! The soul is more amazed every day as she discovers that these divine Persons never leave her anymore. Through this sublime knowing she clearly sees that they are with her always. She perceives their sacred presence in a radically inner place, inside her own depths. She just hasn't learned the language to be able to explain this knowing.

You may think that an experience like this would propel the soul beyond herself, that she would become so absorbed she could focus on nothing else. Actually, when it comes to doing anything relating to serving God, she is more present than ever before. As soon as she finishes such a task, she rests again in that divine companionship. In my opinion, as long as the soul does not give up on God, he will never fail to make his presence known to her in a clear way. The soul has grown confident now that God will never leave her. He has granted her this incredible favor, hasn't he? Why would he allow her to lose this precious gift? Even though the soul is justified in her trust, she walks more consciously than ever, careful not to displease her Beloved in any way.

The first time this presence reveals itself is the clearest and most powerful. And there are other moments when the soul feels this fullness of presence, as well. But if her consciousness of the divine companionship were always that intense, she would never get anything done! It would be impossible to think of anything else or to function and live among other human beings. Yet even if the light of this presence does not always burn quite that clear and bright every time the soul checks, that sweet friendship is there.

We could say that the experience is like being in a sunny room with other people and then someone closes the shutters, plunging the space into darkness. The light by which you had seen the others has been taken away, and you won't be able to see them again until the light comes back. But the absence of light doesn't make you think that the people, too, are gone. So it is with the soul. When the light returns and the soul looks around for her holy companions, will she be able to see them again? This kind of seeing is not in her power. It depends on when our Lord desires to open the shutters of the mind. How great is his mercy! He grants the soul the blessing of never leaving her. He wills for her to understand this perfectly.

Through this wonderful companionship, it seems His Majesty wishes to prepare the soul for the revelation of even more. It's a presence that mitigates any fear she used to have about the other divine favors she experienced. The person I mentioned found herself improved in every way by her association with this invisible company. It seemed to her that in spite of the trials she endured or the business affairs she had to attend to, the essential part of her soul never moved from that room. This made her feel that her soul was divided in some way. Shortly after God granted her the revelation of the three divine Persons, she was going through some severe challenges and she complained about that other part of her soul, as Martha complained of Mary. She pointed out that it was always there enjoying that deep quietude while she herself was left with all her troubles and worries, unable to keep it company.

Maybe it sounds ridiculous to you, friends, but this is really what happens. Although we know, of course, that the soul is all one and not divided, still what I'm referring to is no illusion. It's a very common experience. We can look inside ourselves in such a way that we perceive a clear difference between soul and spirit, even though they are really one and the same. The duality is so subtle that differentiating between their functions can be like trying to distinguish one flavor of the Beloved from another.

It also seems to me that there is a distinction to be made between the soul and the faculties of sense and reason. There is such a multitude of such delicate things inside the soul that it would be presumptuous of me to even try to explain them. If the Lord in his mercy grants us the favor of bringing us home to him at last, we will see everything and understand all the secrets when we get there.

I t's time now to explore the divine and spiritual marriage between God and the soul. This is not a favor that can be fully realized in this life. As long as we have the choice to turn away from God, we run the risk of losing that consummate blessing.

When we first receive this favor, His Majesty shares himself with the soul through a visual revelation of his most sacred humanity. In this way, the soul clearly understands what's happening; she is not ignorant of the fact that she is the recipient of a magnificent gift. This gift will be given to different people in different forms. The Beloved revealed himself to a certain person one day just after she had received communion. He represented himself as Jesus Christ, in all his

splendor and beauty and majesty, just as he was after his resurrection. He told her that it was time for her to take up his
work as her own and he would take her work upon himself as
his. He spoke other words, as well, meant more to be felt than
to be mentioned.

This may sound like nothing new. After all, it's not as if
the Beloved hadn't revealed himself to the soul in that way
before. But this experience was so different that it left this
person utterly bewildered and frightened. For one thing, it
came upon her with tremendous force. For another, the
words he spoke were indescribably potent. Also, he represented himself to her in the innermost depths of her soul,
and she had never before seen a vision in that place. There is
a vast difference between the vision she is given in this
dwelling and all the other visions the soul has ever had. The
distinction between the spiritual betrothal and the divine
marriage is as clearly defined as it would be between two
people who are engaged to be married and two whose lives
are so entwined nothing could ever separate them.

I make comparisons like these because I can't think of
any better ones. But you need to know that there is no more
awareness of the body here than if the soul were not in the
body at all. For her, there is nothing but spirit. The connection between soul and body is even more tenuous in the spiritual marriage itself. This secret union unfolds in the deepest
interior of the soul, which must be the place where God himself dwells. In my opinion, no door is required to enter here. I
say this because up till now all that has happened in the soul

has involved the senses and the faculties, even the appearance of the humanity of the Lord.

Everything about the union of spiritual marriage is unique. The Beloved appears at the center of the soul through a very subtle transcendental vision rather than a visual revelation. The secret that God communicates to the soul here in a single instant is so exalted, the favors he bestows upon her so sublime, and the delight he gives her so sweet that I don't know what to compare it to. All I can say is that it is the will of God to manifest the glory of heaven to the soul in that moment. He does this in a more rarefied manner than is possible through any visual revelation or spiritual consolation.

It's impossible to say anything more that could be understood with words, except that the soul—I mean the spirit of this soul—is made one with God, who is also spirit. God desires to show us how much he loves us by revealing the vast reaches of this love to the soul so that we may praise his greatness. All he wants is to be joined with his creature so completely that they can never be torn apart. He doesn't want to be separated from her!

The melding that happens in the spiritual engagement is less integrated than the union of the spiritual marriage. The two beings who have joined are still frequently separated and return to being things-by-themselves. This is a matter of common observation. The experience of connection to the Beloved passes quickly and afterwards the soul is deprived of his company—or at least she thinks she is.

But in total union no separation is possible. The soul

remains perpetually in that center with her God. We could say that that other union is like pressing two softened candles together so that their twin flames yield a single light. Or we could say that the wick, the wax, and the flame are all the same. But afterwards one candle can be easily separated from the other; now there are two candles again. Likewise, the wick can be withdrawn from the wax.

The spiritual marriage, on the other hand, is like rain falling from the sky into a river or pool. There is nothing but water. It's impossible to divide the sky-water from the land-water. When a little stream enters the sea, who could separate its waters back out again? Think of a bright light pouring into a room from two large windows: it enters from different places but becomes one light.

Maybe this is what Saint Paul meant when he said, "Whoever is joined to God becomes one spirit with him." He was probably referring to the royal marriage, presupposing that His Majesty has entered the soul through divine union. He also says, "For me, to live is Christ, and to die is to gain." The soul, I think, can say the same thing here. This is the place where that little butterfly we've been talking about dies. And she dies with the greatest joy because Christ is now her life.

The more the effects of this vision are manifested, the more obvious its truth becomes. Through certain secret inspirations, the soul clearly realizes that it is God who endows her with life. These inspirations very often come with such vibrancy that their teachings cannot possibly be subjected to doubt. Although they are ineffable, they are exceedingly powerful. The feeling is so overwhelming that sometimes the soul cannot keep herself from uttering such phrases as, "Oh, life of my life! Sustenance that sustains me!" It seems that God is continuously sustaining the soul with streams of milk flowing from the divine breasts. This brings solace to all the inhabitants of the castle. It seems to be the will of the Beloved for these others to enjoy all that the spirit is enjoying. Sometimes that full-flowing river that swallows up the tiny spring of the soul swells and spills over to sustain those whose task it is to serve the groom and his bride in corporeal ways.

If a preoccupied person was suddenly plunged into the water, he would certainly notice. How could he not feel it, no matter how distracted he was? Just so, the soul cannot help but be aware of these holy operations, and with even more certainty. Remember when I said that a great stream of water could never reach us if it didn't have its source somewhere? In this state, it is clear that there is someone in the depths of the soul who shoots these arrows and gives life to this life. There is a sun at the soul's center from which emanates a supernatural light that is transmitted to the faculties. The soul does not move from her center or lose her equanimity. The one who gave peace to the apostles when they were together can give peace to the soul. Divine words take action in the soul and work toward stripping her of worldly attachments, leaving her in a state of pure spirit—uncreated spirit—in heavenly union.

One thing that is certain is that when we empty ourselves of all that is creature, detaching ourselves for love of
the Creator, that same God will fill our souls with himself.
And so one day, while Jesus Christ was praying somewhere
for his disciples—I'm not sure where—he declared that they
were one with the Father and with him, just as Christ our
Beloved is in the Father and the Father is in him. What
greater love can there be than this? We are all included here.
Our Beloved went on to say, "I ask not for my disciples alone
but for all beings." And then he said, "I am in them."

Oh, God help me! How true these words are and how
clearly a soul in a state of prayer sees them and understands
them for herself. How well we would all understand them if
we weren't so unconscious sometimes. The words of Christ,
our Beloved and our Lord, cannot fail. But we can. We can
neglect to prepare ourselves. We can forget to turn away from
everything that obstructs this light. And so when we gaze
into the divine mirror in which our image is engraved, we do
not see our own reflection.

Coming back now to what we were talking about before:
the Beloved brings the soul into his own chamber, which is at
the center of the soul herself. They say that the highest
heaven where the Beloved dwells doesn't move like the other
heavens do. That same stillness cradles the soul who enters
here. The customary motions of the faculties and the imagination used to batter the soul. In this center she is no longer
tossed around. No such stirrings compromise her serenity.

Does it seem like I'm saying that once the soul reaches the place where the Beloved grants her this favor she is certain of liberation and safe from ever falling off the path again? That's not what I mean. Whenever I imply that the soul is secure, please understand it to indicate that this is so only as long as the Divine Majesty holds her hand and she does not offend him.

What I do know for sure is that even when the soul finds herself in this exalted state and even if she endures for years, she doesn't consider herself to be truly safe. She walks more mindfully than ever before, careful not to commit the smallest offense against God. Her desire to serve him has grown more passionate and her habitual confusion and dismay about how little she is able to do for him has intensified. She clearly sees how much more he deserves than what she has been able to give, and this pain is no small cross to bear. It turns out, however, that bearing it is a great service in itself. When a soul suffers in this way, her ultimate delight will be even greater. Penance takes many forms. True penance happens when God takes away her health and strength so that she can no longer offer penance!

I know I have described elsewhere the grief that arises in the soul from her inability to serve in this way. But it's much more severe here. This suffering has its roots in the ground in which the soul herself is planted. A tree growing on the banks of fresh-flowing water is vibrantly alive and yields bountiful fruit. So if the true spirit of the soul has become one with the heavenly waters we've been talking about, why should we be surprised by her longing?

As I was saying, just because the soul sits in perpetual peace does not mean that the faculties of sense and reason do, or the passions. There are always wars going on in the other dwellings of the soul. There is no lack of trials and exhaustion. But these battles rarely have the power anymore to unseat the soul from her place of peace.

This center of our soul—this spirit—is difficult to define. It's hard enough just to believe in it! And so, friends, I don't think I'll subject you to the temptation to doubt what I'm saying on the basis of my ineptitude in describing it. How can the soul suffer trials and still be at peace? I can't explain it. Let me try a couple more analogies. Please God, may they be of some use. But if not, I still know that what I'm saying is the truth!

Here's one: the king is in his palace. There are many conflicts in his kingdom. Painful events are exploding all around him, but he stays where he is, no matter what.

Even though in the other dwellings of the interior castle it is noisy and chaotic and poisonous creatures slither around, no one can enter this innermost chamber and force the soul out of it. The things the soul hears cause her some distress, but they do not compel her to leave. This kind of suffering is not able to disturb her equanimity. The passions have been conquered and are afraid to enter the center of the soul because they would only be further debilitated here.

Here's another: our entire body may hurt, but if our head is healthy the pain in the other parts will not make our head ache.

These metaphors make me laugh at myself. I'm not satisfied with them, but I can't come up with any others. Think whatever you want. What I have said is true.

. 3 .

Now the little butterfly has died of happiness, we could say, filled with the living Christ. She has found her rest at last. What is her new life like? How is it different from her old one? We shall see. The truth of what I have said will be revealed through its results.

One of the outcomes of this transformation is a forgetfulness of self. It's as if the soul ceases to be. She doesn't remember anything about a heavenly afterlife or personal honor. Everything in her is dedicated to honoring God. This is all because of those words His Majesty spoke to her. "Look after what is mine," he said, "and I will look after what is yours." And so the soul isn't worried about a thing. She doesn't give a thought to what might or could happen. She lives in such a strange state of forgetfulness that it's as if she no longer existed or had any desire to exist at all, except insofar as it occurs to her that she may be of some use in exalting God. She would gladly lay down her life if it meant increasing the glory and honor of God by even one degree.

Don't think this means that a person in this state forgets to eat and sleep, friends. It's true that the necessity to do these external things is no small torment to her. But that's not the issue. We're talking about interior matters, here. The real pain lies in the soul's realization that all she can do by her own efforts amounts to nothing. Yet there is no reason on earth that she would willingly neglect to do anything that might possibly be of service to the Beloved.

Another outcome of this transformation is a deep desire to bear burdens for God. But this desire doesn't plague the soul the way it used to. She has become totally surrendered to him. Her only wish is that his will be done. She considers everything he does to be for the best. If it is his will that she suffer, fine. If not, she won't launch into the self-destructive behavior she used to engage in.

When a soul in this state is persecuted, she experiences a profound inner joy. She has attained an unshakable peace. She has absolutely no animosity toward those who mistreat her or whose intention it is to do her harm. In fact, a special love for her persecutors grows inside this soul, to the extent that if she sees that they are in trouble, her heart fills with compassion and she would do anything in her power to relieve them of their affliction. She eagerly commends these people to God. She would rejoice in giving up the favors God has granted her if he would bestow these gifts on her persecutors instead so that they would no longer be inclined to offend our Beloved in any way.

You have already observed the tribulation these souls have endured in their longing to be done with this life and merge with our Beloved. What surprises me is that now they are overcome with an equally fervent desire to serve him, to celebrate him, to benefit any other souls if they possibly can. Not only are they no longer interested in dying, but they have a wish to live for many, many years and suffer the most intense trials if it means that they can contribute to the praising of the Lord in even the smallest way.

If it were to be proven to these souls that leaving the body would mean enjoying God endlessly, they would still remain unmoved. Not even the thought of personally participating in the glory of the saints rekindles their desire to transcend this world. Glory, for them, lies in being able to help the crucified in some manifest way. What hurts them most is to see the way people dishonor the Beloved. So few people seem to be primarily focused on God and detached from everything else.

It's true that a soul in this state sometimes forgets this. She returns to tender thoughts of escaping the exile of this world and basking in unending enjoyment of God—especially when she notices how inefficiently she's able to serve him here. But when she turns back to look inside herself again, she remembers that he is with her always. This renewed awareness of his presence comforts her. With that, she offers His Majesty her will to live. This is the most priceless gift she has to give.

The soul at this stage is no more afraid of death than she would fear a gentle rapture. The same Beloved who once instilled those other desires that used to torment the soul now fills her with this contentment. May he be forever blessed and praised.

The soul doesn't yearn for spiritual gratification anymore. She has His Majesty himself living inside her! The life of Christ was a life of unrelenting adversity. Now he is trying to make ours like his—at least in terms of thwarting our deepest desires. In other areas he tenderly leads us around like weaklings. When he sees that we really need it, he bolsters us with generous fortitude.

This is a soul who is growing increasingly detached from all things, wishing only to be alone or engaged in helping some other soul. She no longer suffers from inner aridity or strife. She dwells in gentle remembrance of our Lord and cultivates the most tender love for him. All she wants to do is praise him!

Whenever the soul becomes distracted, the Beloved himself applies those holy impulses we've talked about to waking her up. It's clear to her that the impulse—I'm not sure what else to call that feeling—comes from deep inside her. Here, the soul experiences it as a soft touch. It arises from neither the mind nor the memory. In fact, it doesn't seem to be the result of anything the soul has done of her own power.

This experience becomes frequent and ordinary, affording the soul the opportunity to observe it carefully. Just as flames fly upward rather than drop down no matter how ferocious the fire, the soul experiences this inner flow as radiating from her center, awakening the faculties along the way.

Even if we gained nothing else from this way of prayer besides a deepening understanding of the special care God expresses by communing so intimately with us and by so clearly calling us to live in him, this would be enough. All the trials the soul endures for the sake of tasting these gently penetrating morsels of the Beloved's love are worthwhile, without a doubt.

You must have experienced this, friends. Whenever we reach the Prayer of Union, the Beloved begins to shower us with his deep caring, as long as we don't forget to honor his ways. As you enter this state, try to remind yourself that this is the innermost chamber where God dwells inside our souls, and then praise him with all your heart. This experience is a love letter from God to you, written with pure love, composed in a secret code meant for you alone. Only you can understand what he is saying and what he is asking of you. You must not, under any circumstances, neglect to reply to His Majesty, even if you're in the middle of a conversation with some people or engaged in other external matters.

Our Beloved will often choose to grant you this favor in public. In that case, your response can be invisible. You answer the call of your God inside yourself. Do what I say.

Make an act of love. Silently exclaim with Saint Paul, "Lord, what will you have me do?" He will teach you many ways of pleasing him. Now is the time. He seems to be listening. His delicate touch stimulates the soul's firm determination to do whatever he is asking her to do.

Remember, there are hardly any more spells of aridity in this dwelling. The inner turmoil that used to shake the soul in the other dwellings has given way to a sustained quietude. The soul has no fear. She doesn't think that this sweet favor could be a trick of the spirit of evil; she is unwavering in her certainty that it comes from God. Don't forget: the faculties and the senses have nothing to do with this place, either. This is a secret place where His Majesty has taken the soul and unveiled himself to her. He would never let the spirit of evil in. All the favors the Beloved shares with the soul here require no contribution from the soul herself, beyond her absolute surrender to God.

In this state of prayer, the Beloved teaches the soul so quietly, so peacefully, it reminds me of the construction of Solomon's Temple where not a sound could be heard. Here in the temple of God, in his innermost dwelling place, God and the soul rejoice in each other, in the deepest silence. There is no reason for the mind to be stirred. It has nothing to seek, nothing to find. The Lord who created the soul is now offering her sanctuary, providing the vantage point of a peephole through which she can gaze at all that is unfolding around her. Sometimes she loses sight of what's happening.

For a moment she can't see anything at all. In my opinion, it's not that the soul has lost her faculties; they just cease to operate here, dazed and amazed.

I myself am quite dazed and amazed to discover that when the soul reaches this stage her raptures cease, except for very occasional occurrences. And even these rare absorptions do not include those transports and flights of the spirit. And they hardly ever occur in public anymore. Nor are they triggered now by moments of devotion. We can look at sacred images, hear spiritual talks, and listen to religious music and it's almost as if nothing had happened. Before, that poor little butterfly was always so frightened that every little thing made her fly away!

Who knows why this has changed? Maybe it's because in this dwelling she has found a place to rest at last. Maybe it's because, after all she has experienced, nothing can scare her anymore. Maybe it's because now she has this constant loving companionship and so she no longer feels alone. I'm not sure what the real reason is, friends. All I know is that when the Beloved brings the soul into this dwelling and begins to reveal to her what there is here, this great weakness of hers that has been such a trial to her and which she could never seem to shake off, is lifted away at last. Maybe it's because the Beloved has strengthened the soul now, expanding and validating her. Maybe he was simply ready to make public what he was doing with the soul in private. Only His Majesty knows why he does what he does. His judgments are inscrutable, transcending anything we can imagine here on earth.

When the soul approaches the Beloved now, he bestows upon her the kiss sought by the bride. And enfolded in this kiss are all the other blessings that come with every degree of prayer that has unfolded along the soul's journey home to him. In my understanding, it is here in this dwelling that all the soul has been longing for is fulfilled. Here the wounded deer is given abundant water to drink. Here the soul delights beneath God's holy tent. Here the dove Noah sent out to see if the storm was over finds the olive branch as a sign that firm ground exists amid the storms and floods of this world.

Oh, Jesus! If only we could find the countless jewels hidden in sacred scriptures to guide us to this deep soul-peace! My God, since you see how desperately we need it, please inspire us to seek it. And if you have already given us peace, please God, in your mercy, do not take it away. Until you have brought us to that place of true peace that never ends, we will always live with that fear. I say "true peace" not because I think that this other peace is not true but because in this life it is always possible for us to turn away from God and for war to break out again.

What does this soul feel when she realizes that she is at risk of losing such a great blessing? This thought makes her walk more mindfully and seek to draw strength from her weakness. She takes full responsibility for her actions so that she will not miss any opportunity to please God. The more favored she is by His Majesty, the more afraid she is of herself. Knowledge of his greatness has highlighted her knowledge of her own imperfection. Her faults feel more serious to her. She goes around like the publican, reluctant to raise her eyes.

Sometimes she wants to die, just so that she'll be safe from occasions for error. But then, because her love for God is so vast, she grows eager once again to live long so that she can serve him more. She entrusts every aspect of who she is to his mercy. There are times when the abundance of favors he gives to her is overwhelming. She is afraid that she will drop like an overladen ship sinking to the bottom of the sea.

Believe me, friends, there is no lack of crosses to bear. But they do not disquiet the soul in this state or steal away her serenity. Storms pass quickly here, like ocean waves, and fair weather soon returns. Then the presence of the Beloved inside of her makes her forget everything else.

May he be forever blessed and praised by all his creatures. Amen.

.4.

I don't want you to think, friends, that the various effects I've been describing always occur in the same way with every soul. This is why, whenever I remember, I say "usually." Sometimes the Beloved leaves souls in their natural state. That's when it seems like all the toxic creatures from the farthest corners of the castle come swarming in to pay the soul back for the time when they were unable to have their way with her.

It's true that this attack usually only lasts for a day or two, at the most. The turmoil is usually triggered by some random event, but through the ensuing tribulation the soul begins to clearly realize that she has an excellent companion by her side. The Beloved has deepened her integrity and strengthened her commitment so that nothing can move her to waver in her service to him or deviate from her good intentions. If anything, her determination seems to increase. The soul is mindful to cultivate stillness so that she won't be easily deflected from her course.

This kind of disturbance is a rare thing by now, but the Beloved uses it as a way to remind the soul of who she is and to refine her humility. It also heightens her awareness of the great favor she is receiving from God and the deep debt of gratitude she owes him, which inspires her to praise him.

Nor should you assume, friends, that just because the soul in this state is fiercely determined not to commit any imperfection for anything on earth that that means she succeeds in avoiding it. She makes many mistakes. She doesn't mean to, of course. And the Beloved gives her a lot of help in resisting negative impulses. By this time, the soul considers herself to be mostly free from the possibility of grave error, but she still misses the mark in small ways. It torments the soul to think that she might be unconsciously doing wicked things. And seeing other people go astray also causes her pain.

Do you remember how the scriptures mention certain people, like Solomon, who seemed to be so deeply favored by the Lord, communing intimately with His Majesty? Then look what happened! We may harbor the hope that we ourselves are not among those who are still in danger of sliding off the path, but the truth is we must remain ever-vigilant about this. Let she among you who feels most sure of herself fear most. "Blessed is the man in awe of the Lord," says David. May His Majesty protect us always. Let us beseech him not to allow us to offend him. This is the greatest security we can have. May he be forever praised. Amen.

It will be a good thing, friends, if I tell you why the Beloved grants so many blessings in this world. Of course, if you pay attention, this will be evident from the effects they produce. Still, I want to say more about it so that you don't think the reason for these favors is to gratify the soul. That notion would be seriously erroneous. The greatest favor the Lord could offer us would be to give us the opportunity to emulate the life his beloved Son lived. What I know for sure is that these blessings are intended to fortify our weakness so that we can follow in his footsteps and feel his suffering.

We have always seen that those who walked closest to Christ were those who faced the most severe difficulty. Think about what his glorious Mother went through, and his blessed disciples. How do you think Saint Paul endured such terrible trials? His life is a model for the wondrous effects of a contemplative path and of visions that come from the Beloved and not from the delusions of our own imaginations or the deceptions of the spirit of evil. Do you think Saint Paul lost himself indulging in these delights, engaging in nothing else? You know well that he didn't take a day of rest. From what we understand, he didn't even let down at night, since it was at night that he had to earn his living.

There is a story I have always found moving: Saint Peter was escaping from prison when Christ appeared and told him, "I am on my way to be crucified again." Every time I read that part during our services I draw special comfort from it. What effect did this favor from Christ have on Saint Peter? What did he do next? He went straight to his own death. And it was no small mercy that the Beloved provided him with someone to take his life.

Oh, my friends! The Beloved is dwelling in this soul in a unique way. She should relinquish all thought of resting and let go of any craving for personal honor or recognition. If the soul is so deeply with God, then she should not think much about herself. She will be exclusively concerned with finding ways to please him and showing him how much she loves him. This, my friends, is the purpose of prayer. This is the reason for the spiritual marriage. Good works are born from this. Good works.

Remember, good works are a sign of God's blessing. What benefit comes from me isolating myself, absorbed in making acts of love to our Lord, proposing and promising to do all kinds of wonders in his service, if as soon as I leave my private sanctuary I find the least opportunity to do the exact opposite of my lofty intentions? Actually, I am wrong to question this. The truth is, everything having to do with God does us good. Even though we may turn out to be too weak to carry out our bold resolutions, sometimes His Majesty will give us the power to do so. Of course, this in itself may be a great burden to us. When he sees a timid soul, he presents her with some kind of severe trial that opposes her own will, and then he helps her to bear it in such a way that she grows from the experience. The soul understands this later and it alleviates her fear, allowing her to offer herself to him more willingly.

When I implied that our private conversations with God yield a meager profit, I only meant in comparison to the great benefit of aligning our deeds in the world with the words we generate in prayer. What we cannot accomplish all at once, we can do little by little. If the soul wishes for her prayer to be fruitful, let her give up her attachment to her own way and open to the divine will. In the numerous nooks and crannies of the spiritual life, there will be plenty of opportunities to do this.

Reflect deeply on this. I cannot overemphasize its importance. Fix your eyes on the crucified and everything else will seem insignificant. Since Christ demonstrated his love by doing such amazing things and suffering so radically for us, how can your mere words be enough to please our Beloved? Do you know what it means to be truly spiritual? It means becoming a slave to God. We are branded with the sign of the cross. It is the token that we have given him our freedom. Now he can offer us as servants to the whole world, as he offers himself. This does us no harm. In fact, he is granting us a great boon.

Until we surrender to this divine slavery, we cannot expect to make much progress. The foundation of the whole building is humility. If you are not truly humble, the Beloved will not build very high, for your own sake. Otherwise it would all come tumbling to the ground.

And so, friends, if you want to lay a decent foundation, strive to be the least among you. Offer yourself as a slave to God and try to find ways to serve and soothe your companions. This will be of even more value to you than to them; the stones that support you will be firmly laid and your castle will not fall.

You must remember not to build on prayer and contemplation alone. Unless you strive to live the virtues, you will never grow beyond the stature of spiritual dwarves. Pray that in that case it will only be a matter of not growing, rather than of shrinking! As you know, he who fails to move forward slides backward. I believe that love doesn't let a soul be content with staying in the same place for long.

It may seem to you that I am referring to beginners here, and that those of you who have progressed beyond the earliest stages can relax about this. I have already told you: any rest these souls get happens only on the inside. They have less and less external peace, and less need for it. What do you think is the reason for those inspirations aspirations, really that I've talked about? What about those messages the soul transmits from her innermost center to the beings in the other dwellings and those outside the castle? Is it so they can fall asleep? No, absolutely not! The soul struggles harder to maintain the faculties, senses, and the whole of the body in a state of heightened awareness than she ever did when she herself was personally identified with their suffering. She didn't understand the great benefit of trials, then. Maybe it was her very suffering that led her to this center where her wondrous companion gives her greater strength than she's ever had.

Here on earth, says David, among the holy we shall be holy. And so we cannot doubt that if we are made one with the Strong One through the supreme union of spirit with spirit, we will gather the strength we need. We will come to appreciate the fortitude that supported the saints in their suffering and their death.

It is clear that the soul applies the strength she has gathered to helping all the beings in the castle—even the body, which often feels insignificant. The soul has tasted the wine from this cellar where the Spouse has brought her and will not let her leave. And from this wine strength flows back into the weak body, just as on a mundane level the food we take into our stomach strengthens the whole body and energizes the head.

The soul has a hard time in this life. The more she goes through, the more her inner strength increases and so the more her inner battles intensify. No matter how much she does, she is always capable of doing more and nothing she does seems to matter. This must be what gave rise to the great penances of the saints—especially the glorious Magdalene who had lived a life of sheer luxury. And then there was that hunger our father Elijah had for the honor of God. This same hunger drove Saint Dominic and Saint Francis to bring souls to God and inspire them to praise him. Although they were forgetful of themselves, I assure you they must have suffered greatly.

This is what I would like for us to strive for, friends. We should engage in prayer—thirst for it, even—not because it feels good, but because it gives us the strength we need to be of service. There is no reason to blaze any new trails; we'll only waste valuable time. The notion of acquiring these favors from God by a different path than the one Christ and his disciples followed may be an interesting one to ponder, but you can forget about it.

Believe me, Martha and Mary need to come together to offer hospitality to Christ. They need to have him present with them at all times. They must not neglect to give him something to eat. How can Mary, seated constantly at his feet, give him anything unless her sister helps her? The souls we bring to him are his food. May we do everything we can to help other beings to rejoice in the Lord always.

You might question a couple of things, here. One is that Christ did say that it was Mary who had chosen "the better part." The point is, Mary had already done the work of Martha, showing Christ the depth of her love by washing his feet with priceless perfume and wiping them dry with her hair. Do you think it would have been an insignificant sacrifice for a woman of such noble stature to wander those streets—maybe even alone, since her ardent love made her heedless of propriety—and barge into a house whose threshold she had never crossed before, and then afterwards have to put up with the criticisms of the Pharisee, not to mention all the other things she had to endure? What the people saw was a woman undergoing a radical life transformation. What the malicious among them reacted to was her friendship with the Christ they so fiercely hated, the noticeable change in her appearance, and her obvious desire to live a holy life. All of this led them to comment on the way she lived before. Think about how blithely we gossip now about people far less notorious than the Magdalene was considered to be then. Imagine what she must have had to deal with!

I tell you, friends, this "better part" was the fruit of many trials and sacrifices. Even just seeing her Lord despised must have been unbearable to her. And then there were all the trials she endured after his death, not to mention the sheer anguish of having to live without him. So you see, Mary was not always just basking in the light of contemplation at the feet of the Beloved.

The other objection you might raise is that you yourself do not have the skill to guide souls to God. You are not teachers or preachers like the apostles were. You would gladly do it, but you don't know how. I know I have addressed this question in places other than this Castle, but I think it's worth going over it again here, since I believe that it is God who is planting the wish in your hearts and that's why it's occurring to you. Remember when I told you that the spirit of evil sometimes stimulates us with grandiose desires? This is so that we will avoid putting our attention on the tasks at hand and serving our Beloved in feasible ways. Instead, we content ourselves with having wished for the impossible.

Prayer alone can do a lot of good for the people you pray for. Beyond that, it's not necessary to try to help the whole world. Concentrate on your own circle of companions who need you. Then, whatever you do will be of greater benefit.

Do you think that your deep humility, your self-sacrifice, your bountiful charity and commitment to being of service to all beings is meaningless? The fire of your love for God enkindles other souls. You awaken them through the living example of your own virtues. This is no small service. It is great service! It's highly pleasing to the Lord. Do what you can do. His Majesty will understand that you yearn to do much more. And he will reward you as if you had guided a thousand unknown souls to him.

You might say that serving those in our sphere doesn't do much good since they are already skillfully walking a spiritual path. Who are you to judge this? They can do better! And the better they do, the more pleasing their praises to God will be and the more effective their prayers for their neighbors.

And so, my friends, I will end by suggesting that we avoid building towers without foundations. The Beloved looks less at the grandeur of our deeds than at the love with which we perform them. If we do what we can, His Majesty will help us to do more each day. It's best not to start off exhausted by impossible efforts. This life is short—maybe even shorter than most of us think. Let's offer the Beloved whatever inner and outer sacrifice we can give. His Majesty will unite our offerings with the sacrifice the Son made to the Father on the cross. Then, even if our deeds are small, they will be made great through the greatness of our love for God.

May it please His Majesty, my friends, that we all reach the place where we may praise him ceaselessly. Through the merits of the Son who lives and loves forever and ever, may he give me the grace to carry out some of what I have told you about here. Amen.

I confess that I am deeply confused and so I ask you through the same Beloved to remember this poor creature in your prayers.

EPILOGUE

Even though I began this writing with great reluctance,
now that I am finished I must admit that the work has
brought me great joy. And while my labor was small, I count
it as well spent. Considering the strict commitment to simplicity many of you have made, the harsh conditions in which
some of you live, and the lack of opportunity for recreation,
I hope it will be a source of real consolation for you to take
your delight in this interior castle. You can walk here whenever you feel like it, without having to ask permission from
anyone.

It's true that, no matter how strong you think you are,
you may not be able to gain entrance to all the dwellings

through your own efforts. Only the Lord of the castle himself can let you in. So, if you meet with any resistance, I advise you not to try to enter by force. This will only displease him, and he will not be inclined to admit you in the future.

He is a great lover of humility. If you don't consider yourself ready to enter even the third dwelling, he will likely give you speedy access to the fifth! After that, you will be able to serve him by touching down in each dwelling again and again until he brings you to that innermost chamber he keeps for himself. This is a place you do not ever have to leave. Of course, sometimes your spiritual director will call you out. This is all right. The Beloved is content for you to honor her wishes as his own. And even if you are often drawn away from this center, you will always find the door open when you return.

Once you have been shown how to enjoy this castle you will find rest in everything, even in the things that challenge you most. You will hold in your heart the hope of returning to the castle, and no one can take that from you.

Although I have only spoken of seven dwellings here, each one contains many others above, below, and all around with lovely gardens and fountains and labyrinths. Each place is filled with such delightful things that you will want to lose yourself in praising the great God who created the soul in his own image and likeness.

If you find any good thing in this book and it helps you to know God better, you can be sure that it is His Majesty who has said it to make you happy. Any bad thing you may have found has been said by me.

Through the intense desire I have to be of some use in inspiring you to serve my God and Beloved, I ask that you praise His Majesty with all your heart each time you read this. Beseech him to awaken all beings and bring light to those who are lost. And please ask him to pardon my imperfections and set me free.

Perhaps, by the mercy of God, I will have been released from this exile by the time you read this. It is only after my work has been examined by men of learning that it will be allowed to reach your hands. If I have said anything wrong, it's because I didn't know any better. In all things, I submit to the authority of the Church in which I live and die. It is from her that I draw my faith and to her I promise my life.

May God our Beloved be forever blessed and praised. Amen.

This writing was finished in the convent of Saint Joseph of Avila in the year 1577 on the eve of the feast of Saint Andrew, for the glory of God who lives and reigns forever and ever. Amen.

ABOUT THE AUTHOR

Mirabai Starr first encountered the work of Saint Teresa of Avila over twenty years ago while studying the work of sixteenth-century religious reformer Saint John of the Cross. The two mystics were close friends and confidants, each heavily influencing the other's work. Despite this close relationship, John and Teresa approached their faith and writing in radically different ways. While John's calm, austere style was balanced by a smoldering inner passion for God, Teresa's flamboyant outer expressiveness opened to a profound inner quietude.

Translating *The Interior Castle* shortly after the sudden death of her teenaged daughter, Jenny, provided Mirabai with unexpected solace. Teresa's deep compassion and her gentle reminders of our ever-present relationship with the Divine offered palpable comfort and inspiration. An active speaker, as well as writer and translator, Mirabai uses the teachings of the Spanish mystics to help guide people suffering from grief and loss to use their experiences in positive ways.

In addition to her translations, Mirabai has written award-winning short stories and essays for various spiritual and literary publications. She teaches Philosophy and Religious Studies at the University of New Mexico, Taos. Mirabai lives in the mountains of Northern New Mexico with her husband, Jeff Little.

Metaphors v the butterflys
+ the wax+ seal - 5th - 2